THE LAST OF WILL

THE LAST OF WILL

SHERYL BENKO

FIRST EDITION

Cover design and artwork by Leon Joosen

ISBN 978-0-9996888-0-9 (paperback)
ISBN 978-0-9996888-1-6 (e-book)

For the loved ones who now walk in a new life …
but still have a laugh along the way.

CONTENTS

THE LAST OF WILL

1

LAST WEDNESDAY

Three words. That's all it took to send the whole scenario into a tailspin. Not that things were looking too promising up to that point. It was only a matter of time before the other shoe would drop, because that's how physics works. Supposedly.

"Excuse me??"

Two words. That was enough to signal the start of the spiral. Of course, when spouted by a mother on her last nerve, the phrase can almost drag out to three words. *"Ex cuuuuse me??"* Two and a half, at least.

Look, I'm the first to acknowledge that since I'm fifteen, most people assume I'm naturally a complacent, disinterested teenager. Fine, I'll give you that. But don't expect me to care so little that I'm gonna let the blatant truth slide by when someone desperately needs to be smacked upside the head with reality.

Frankly, there was no hope of dressing it up to make it pretty, even if I'd wanted to. After months of dancing around the obvious, the whole maneuver had become a pitifully useless exercise ... not to mention, *way* boring. So I figured a little brutal honesty couldn't hurt. That should have been my first clue to step back. I mean, stop for a second and think of how many of your life-altering choices and whacked-out haircuts and twisted relationships seemed like good ideas at the time. I don't need the gory details—just nod.

Sure, I get it that my life experience is rather limited, so why should you listen to me? Hey, I'm not arguing with you. Unlike other teenagers, I don't claim to know everything. If I actually knew everything, then way too many annoying people would be bugging me for advice all day, and who needs that grief? Even God took a day off.

But here's the thing—aside from all the stuff I don't know yet, I do know enough to recognize that some choices are just destined to fail, no matter what. It's like psychological dodgeball. You might start out making some good decisions, but eventually, you get down to the scrawny, awkward and wheezy varieties, resulting in a selection that may or may not contribute to your win column. So despite what the coach says, failure is totally an option.

Even if we regularly end up on the smart team, we're all intellectual weaklings at times, since the universe needs stupidity to balance things out. And there's plenty of it to go around. Like, idiotic politicians who forget to zip up and end up screwing themselves, which—let's be real— defeats the whole purpose.

Thickheaded criminals are notoriously entertaining, and living proof that some people get a free pass in the whole "walking and chewing gum" department.

And then there is the cornerstone of our society: dumb teenagers, of which I have clearly proven to be one at the moment; which explains this conversation in my head, although I still can't fathom how you got in here to watch this trainwreck unfold. Seriously, I don't recall sending out invitations. But since you're here, try to keep up.

Where was I? Oh yeah, the stupidity thing ...

The scary ones are the people who *are* smart, but who make surprisingly dopey choices. Politicians and some criminals qualify for this category, but the most pronounced example of a teenager I've known was Linus Beadleman, who went to my junior high school. On the one hand, he was blessed with this really spongy brain that could absorb, like, the most ridiculous amount of knowledge that he could probably win *Jeopardy* without even breaking a sweat. On the other hand, he was cursed with a name like "Linus Beadleman."

Somewhere in the middle, it seemed he never quite grasped the whole concept of coexisting, in general. My grandma would have called him "book smart and life stupid," since even though he spoke English, his words generally sailed over most people's heads. I asked to borrow his ruler one time, and all I remember is a dizzying dissertation about measurement conversion and how to remove splinters with a drawing compass. Good thing my chair was against the wall; it was the only thing stopping me from keeling over.

Then Linus just dropped off the map one day. The rumor mill said he went to Switzerland for a sex change, and came back as Vera Fernlander, who showed up midyear. But if that's true, then somebody should demand their money back, since she's a total ditz. Let's face it, if you're gonna rebuild the engine, why lose the high-tech dashboard?

Personally, I think he joined a cult. Probably nothing too harsh or off the charts—just an incoherent brochure. On a scale of one to ten cultdom … maybe a four.

Sorry, I'm railing. Getting back to my mom …

As long as you can identify a bad decision as soon as you've made it, there's usually a limited time to dig yourself out. A tiny window to salvage things before they hit rock bottom. Usually. Unless—like me—you choose the path of least reward. In this case, that would be called "honesty."

"Dad's losing it." There, I said it. Release the hounds.

I expected an immediate retort. Something a little pithy or sarcastic. She's good at that. Snappy comebacks are kinda her thing. I gotta say, though, the audible gasp was a little unnerving. Not that I haven't heard it before. Trust me, it's frequently part of the repertoire, but is prone to hovering around "orange," and only occasionally tipping into "red." To play that card so early meant one of two things: either she was mentally tapped out, or the life was literally being sucked out of her.

Then, the noticeable beat of hesitation. If it had lasted a few seconds longer, I either would have bolted or called "911," since the blood filling her face looked like Mount Vesuvius about to spew. But the arching of the eyebrow meant words were coming, so she hadn't fully clocked out. I inwardly lied to myself, expecting her to appreciate the reality check.

"Greer Sarazen! How *dare* you say that about your father!"

Fine. I was wrong. I suck at this. And yes, my name is Greer. We'll get back to that later. Time for a new tactic.

"Oh, right! Like he hasn't gone a little wacko these last few months??"

Genius. *Putting the onus on the one who disagrees with you.* Make them state their case, instead. Then sit back and enjoy.

Again, the bloated pause. The smell of victory hung in the air. Her clenched jaw and nervous tic were classic. She knew it was true, and was fighting everything in her being to not surrender. It was like that moment on every one of the bazillion crime shows, when the cops break it to the suspect that their spit was on the murder weapon, and DNA doesn't lie. Time to take the perp walk.

"Well," she started, trying to save face, "he's been going through a rough patch."

Nice warm-up; now let's see it spin.

"But he'll get a job soon and be back to normal in no time."

Hmmm. The judges were shaking their heads. A 5.6 on technical, but .2 on artistry.

I debated whether to respond and shatter her bubble of self-delusion, or just let it go. True to form, she made the choice for me, by walking away and getting the last word. Maybe it's because she legitimately thought she was right. Or maybe she wasn't too sure, and figured the silence wouldn't say anything she didn't want to hear.

Like I said, I'm only fifteen, so people don't expect me to know too much about life. But I do observe. And occasionally listen. And when you do listen, you learn that silence screams louder than any argument.

*

They should provide instructions. A pamphlet or something. But of course, they don't. Even when my sister got her first mind-numbing summer job at "Herman's Hacienda" (which she still bitches about to this day) they gave her a manifesto of paperwork. When you start working somewhere, all they want to do is inform you. "Here are the rules." "This is the procedure." "That is considered sexual harassment, so just don't go there." Of course, there's always that stable of geniuses who don't bother to read the paperwork when they start a new job ... but that's a whole other tirade.

Good luck getting any information when your job is pulled out from under you. I would think that's when you need pointers the most. Not even so much for the person who lost the job, because when you're that happy individual, no doubt you just want to backhand every corporate schmuck within arm's length, after being informed you have to train your replacement.

No, the instructions are for the family, or whoever lives within earshot of the recently unemployed. Step-by-step guidelines to pinpoint what you're up against on any given day. You know, stuff like "How to Talk to the Newly Jobless." "What *NOT* to Say." "Hiding Flammables and Other Impulse Purchases."

Is it *really* that much to ask? Just a little shout-out to the home team. But, no. You get nothin'. They might as well have fired the person's entire social circle, because ultimately, you've all been kicked to the curb. So you're left to figure out things on your own. Basically, you lie to yourself, inwardly convinced that you're helping, while you mine the depths of their despair and just hope to not jack 'em up any further. The trick is to be creative and resourceful when you're getting no reinforcement from your subject.

Here's a tip: mirrors are handy. Not only do they scare off the undead, but they can help identify the dead when it's not too clear what's in front of you. First rule: check if they're breathing. Yardsticks and packaging tape are key, if you need to rig up a test strip because you don't want to get too close. In this case, my grandma would probably claim "I wouldn't touch that with a ten-foot pole." But we don't have that many yardsticks, so I had to improvise.

Be selective about the angle, since you may need a quick retreat. Slide in slowly, so you don't wake the sleeping giant. Then see if any mist or drool shows up on the glass.

That was the plan. Okay, not a distinctly grand plan, but it was a plan of some kind, and damn if I knew what else to do. He was just sitting there. Staring off into space with that zoned-out expression. I couldn't even tell if he was blinking. I saw some movement, but then there was, like, this "gnat" thing buzzing around, so it may have been an involuntary spasm or something. Supposedly, dead bodies exude built-up gas, so that could have been the rank odor. But all dads fart, so wafting fumes are pretty much commonplace, and could imply that he's very much alive. I had to be sure.

All signs indicated that something had gone terribly awry. The half-scribbled, illegible notes; the frozen hand on the computer mouse; the bedhead and sorry bathrobe that may have been housing small animals; the resume with fossilized coffee stains. All the earmarks of a wannabe explorer staring into the dank cavern of his future, and running smack into The Donner Party.

And then...there it was. The mist. A little bit, anyway, and then the drool. He was totally alive. Just staring at internet job listings with that glazed, vapid look. Like somebody glued to a cat video marathon. I had to get him to safety, before he became roadkill.

"Dad?"

Nothing but a blink.

"Dad!"

That's it, up the volume. It's like Americans traveling in a foreign country. Whenever somebody doesn't speak English, we just talk louder, thinking that'll cure everything.

And then came a gurgle. Proof of life. The logical part of my brain was pleading, "Baby step!" But there was precious little time to waste. Screw logic.

"You all right?" I asked.

Let me just acknowledge, here and now—you blow off logic, and it will always bite you in the ass. I offer Exhibit A ...

A head turn, with those same hollow eyes looking at me. Now I was the one who was petrified. Imagine Medusa jumping on your computer and the bitch refuses to log off. Oh, happy day.

"Huh?" he grunted.

I just wanted to get it over with, because I had no idea what I was doing. And I'd peed my pants a little.

Here's the short version: Dad was an accountant, he was good at his job, and did our taxes every year and the Feds haven't busted down the door yet, so I guess he did something right. But those dicks at his company laid off a ton of people last year, and Dad was one of them. He's been slowly going insane ever since. Maybe not clinically, but there's definitely a few new squirrels in his attic now.

See, Dad was a bit of a workaholic, so aside from losing the paycheck (which practically flatlined Mom), his identity more or less vanished, too. It's like he doesn't know what to do with himself. Bottom line is, he worked hard, and he deserved better. What he got was a kick in the gnads, and he's still doubled over.

Even though I'd heard that Herman was looking for a new dishwasher at the Hacienda, I didn't mention it.

Things were already a big enough drag.

2

LAST STRAW

"When the hell did he discover social networks??"

It was a legitimate question, seeing as our dad had rarely ventured onto anything past business listings on a search engine. Even online porn held no appeal for him ... that we know of. Ignorant bliss is my vote in that department.

"This is dangerous," Liv surmises. "He's been spending *way* too much time on that computer."

Liv's my older sister. As you can see, she got the cool name, which justifies the conversation we're having.

"Why should he care if you modified your name a little? It's *your* name, after all. You own it."

My point, exactly. However, the original purchaser felt it was still under warranty.

"Possession is nine-tenths of the law, you know," Liv argues, as if we need any reminders of her ex-boyfriend, Monty, who learned that the hard way.

Liv loves to devise arguments. It's one of her specialties, really. So she's mastered the art of going an entire twelve rounds with Mom, while I usually take a dive to mercifully end it.

"You can't let this one go," she insists. "Invasion of privacy is a breach of the owner-tenant covenant. Why do you think I moved out?"

Um, let's see … Liv is nineteen, in college, with a loser boyfriend whose three regular purchases are beer, condoms, and pork rinds—in that order. Do the math. But she has a valid point.

As for the current drama, the whole thing started because, regrettably, in Dad's massive time on the computer, he had stumbled upon a few new sites—one of them tragically being my "Facebook" page.

"When did you change your name to *Gi?*" he wailed.

Let me set the scene … I had gone to the kitchen, while committing the sacrilege of keeping my laptop open in a common area. Who knew Dad was going to venture out of his mental hole long enough to reach the hallway? I didn't quite hear the full extent of what he said, since the high-pitched warble had more or less mutated through the walls prior to reaching my ears. But I caught enough to know that it wasn't good. You gotta understand—I'm not a confrontational person by nature, but I do realize it's best to brace before walking into the unknown. Grabbing a steak knife seemed rather extreme, so I stuffed my mouth with saltines, in case I had to buy time with an unintelligible response.

"Wha?" I mumbled, inching into the den of doom.

"Your name. On your web page. *Gi?*"

Clipped sentences are never good. They not only imply a level of controlled anger, but also show that the person is only mildly trying to make sense of something they have no use for. They're not interested in details. They want answers. And they'd better come quick.

"Whassa big de-awl?" I slurred, the saltines steadily building my water retention.

"You want to be named after a karate suit?"

Hmmm. Hadn't considered that angle. I was just aiming for the phonetic spelling of the letter "G." But now that you mention it ... "Gi" is kinda cool, in a Ninja sort of way. And given that my tongue was now the size of a blowfish, loose attire may be in order, since gout couldn't be far behind. But Ninjas are so yesterday, and despite my futile hopes, the saltines had dissolved, so I was running out of options.

"*Gi* could mean other things," I reasoned.

"Uh huh," Dad agreed. "Let's see ... 'g, i' ... Soldier. Gastrointestinal. Glycemic index. Stop me when anything grabs your fancy."

Copy that, I got it. Impulse purchases are not good when picking a name.

"It's just ... I wanted a change," I explained. "I'm growing, developing. Becoming my own person. It's important that I be true to myself. So I wanted to start fresh."

Wow, I even impressed myself with that one. It sounded mature, rational, even spiritual. Well done, you.

"Huh?" he retorted.

"It's just ..." I tried to find the words to come next. But only one could truly drive home the point. "*Greer.*"

He stared at me, wanting more. So I plodded on.

"I just don't ... feel it."

The stare continued.

"It's not my thing," I said.

"It's not a thing, it's your name," he frowned.

You know those moments when you should probably stop talking? But for whatever reason, you keep going? Yeeeahhhhh ...

"Oh, it's a thing all right," I dug in. "A big thing. Like a huge, gaping wound kind of thing, with lots of ... *salt* ... dumped in it every day. Which makes it an even bigger, stinging, cavernous ... *thing*. And that thing needs to not *be* a thing anymore. That's the thing."

Dad struggled to be barely interested. "I have no idea what you're saying."

"It doesn't work for me."

That's the simplest explanation I could muster. Not as colorful as others, but to the point. And a whole lot more forgiving than what I coulda said.

A long pause. Then, a breakthrough ... of sorts.

"Well ..." he offered, "What else would work? Besides Gi?"

Nobody told me there'd be a quiz. I had to think fast.

"Um ... I don't know. How 'bout ... *Ger?*"

Yep, I totally just made that up. A little angry, but still original. Or so I thought.

"Now you want to be named after a hut in Mongolia?"

A Mongolian hut? Frick, how much useless trivia does this guy know? Wait ... Mongolians are sorta cool, right? Was that Genghis Khan? I tend to doze in History.

"You're not calling yourself 'Ger.' Period."

Great, he had to throw in verbal punctuation. Could this get any worse?

"Wait 'til I tell your mother."

Boom! Officially worse.

Just for the record, it's not like I hate my name. I'd just appreciate a little variation, that's all. Take Liv—her full name is "Olivia," so she's got some options: "Liv," "Ollie," "Vi." You get the picture. Just a little something to break the monotony, depending on your mood. Even Dad has that option, since his full name is "William," but he goes by "Will." I told him to try "Liam" while he recharges, but he didn't bite. But at least the option is there.

Options are good. Options give us hope. They keep us sane, because they give us a chance of not blowing it … before we eventually blow it.

There are two types of suggestions: the ones that are made to help the rest of us, and ones that are made to help the one doing the suggesting. It's 6:37a.m. on a Tuesday and I've barely had time to pee, let alone clean the crustees outta my eyes long enough to find something less than hideous to wear to school. Take a guess which version of suggestion is being lobbed at me.

"You want me to do *what?*"

"Take your father to his job interview today," Mom says.

Yes, those exact words. So I dissect.

"*Take* …? Does that mean …?"

The pregnant pause. This one's going full-term. Then … the infamous huff-sigh, one of her patented moves.

"Yes, you can drive him."

SCORE!! Here I will dare include the ever-so-remote possibility that by some realm of comprehension, there is—on rare occasions—a third type of suggestion that nature throws us as a consolation prize for all the sucky things we've had to endure at times. This type of suggestion I hereby christen "the one that is intended to help the 'Suggestor,' but instead proves ever so prime for the 'Suggestee.'" The Suggestee, in this case, being ... *moi.*

For once, destiny has taken pity on me and locked in a scenario where Mom has no choice but to turn over the car keys without the usual knock-down-drag-out drama. Now, hit pause for a sec. Fact-check: Mom is a florist and owns this cute little shop that's somehow stayed afloat while our family finances squeak by from month-to-month ... which brings us to today. See, while things slow down at other companies, the two sure bets in the floral world are weddings and funerals. Or, as Mom puts it, "Love and death never go out of business."

That doesn't mean it's been an easy ride. Not at all. Since Dad lost his job, Mom's had to lay off most of her employees and is basically running the place by herself. She had massive guilt about the whole thing, even though she kept them on longer than she could readily afford. But the bills stacked up, and over time, she had to let them go. It was harsh.

Anyway, today she's got some big meeting with a potential client for some Bridezilla society wedding. Major payday if she nails it. So she swallows her pride and calls up second team to pinch-hit. Which makes it my lucky day. Done. I win. You heard right. *I. Totally. Win.*

Since I only have my learner's permit, any invitation to drive is like seeing a unicorn on a key chain: beyond belief, and not something you shut up about.

Turns out, Dad has a job interview this morning, and Mom feels like he's too spaced out to be left in charge of heavy machinery. I know that sounds a little dramatic, but considering that I had to check his vitals with a yardstick and hand mirror, at this point, I'd vote to make shaving permissible only on an "as needed" basis. Driving would just be inviting a lawsuit.

Of course, I can't readily show my inner elation to my mom because, after all, that's part of the precarious charm of the third type of suggestion. The Suggestor is, by definition, already screwed, and the Suggestee knows it. But playing that card too early could sabotage the whole "mano y mano" aspect of the moment, and give the upper hand back to the Suggestor, who could renege in a fit of bitterness. Cooler heads must prevail … at least long enough to get the car keys in hand.

"Um … what about school?" I ask.

Honestly, sometimes my innate brilliance is more than I can bear. I pretend to be concerned enough to bring it up, when all the while, I couldn't care less and would die that much happier with one less day of school to crush my spirit.

"I'll get you excused," she allows. "For the morning."

Figures. I knew the whole turn of events had to go south at some point. But I'm all too glad to get out of Geometry and the agony of World History. I mean, yeah, some vaguely interesting stuff happened along the centuries, but all I remember after a chapter is that most wars are about land or religion, most geniuses come off as initially crazy, and most conquerors are shorter than you'd expect. Three constants that never really change.

Bear in mind that I just won the car keys (turf war), crazily asked about school (secretly genius), and I'm fifteen, so am still growing (variable height). There's no need to go to class, since evidently, I know everything I need to know to apply these principles to my life.

That is, until Dad gets in the car. I haven't taken Psychology yet, or I might relish the weirdness.

First, he just sits there, which is good on the surface but more than a little unnerving, since I can't even guess what's churning in that head of his. But since we're both too lethargic to sort it out, we just give up on conversation.

Then, he spends about twenty-five minutes (since I'm taking the slow route to milk my driving time) shuffling, paper clipping, proofreading, reshuffling, and clipping his resume. Sure, crunching numbers all day could make anybody a robot after a while. But since Dad doesn't appear to have a "reboot" button, I just have to bite my tongue and watch this spectacle unfold, in case he has some unseen, turbo-charged robot arm that could muzzle me in a flash if I dare make a snide remark. As fun as it would be to use that gizmo on certain people, I don't want to be the test case.

But then, I see it … the real instrument of my demise. A stapler. By design, they're useful tools. But when user error is involved, they can leave a mark.

He whips it out like a samurai sword, its metal glistening from the sun on the windshield. I halfway expect his words to not match his mouth movements, but since he's not saying anything, there's no real metric to gauge the madness … except for the fact that the guy is brandishing a friggin' stapler.

Okay, first of all, who carries one of those things around as a necessity? Think about it … how often is a stapler on your "out the door" checklist? Let's review. Gum? Check. Cell phone? Check. Lucky penny you found outside the beer tent of the music festival your parents still don't know about and you will forever regard as your crowning underage social achievement? Check.

But a stapler? What the "f"?

As we get closer to the building, he stares straight ahead, like he's taking a visual survey of what may or may not become his life for however many years ahead.

I park with such stunning proficiency that no one could ding the doors if they wanted to, which is ridiculously impressive, considering that you need a can opener to get out of most compact spots. But do I get kudos? Any parking props at all? No. Still the forward stare.

"Um … we're here," I say, in a flimsy attempt to keep the universe spinning.

He slowly removes the paper clip from his resume, and holds up the stapler. His hand loosely grips around it, with all the best intentions. But like a one-hit wonder band, the moment goes nowhere fast. Inwardly, I imagine he's ready to rage against anything and everything for all the stress and anxiety of the last several months. Outwardly, he's just too tired to make a fist. Or his robot arm is out of batteries. So the stapler sits idle.

I think about asking if he's okay, but I know he's not. Why belabor the point? He was already damaged enough before the stapler, so I decide it's time to disarm him, to keep the situation from imploding.

If you've ever had to do it, you know that saving someone from themselves is a noble—if not particularly pretty—task, so the actual maneuvering is anything but graceful. But I'm able to get the stapler into my hand and, more importantly, out of his.

I staple his resume together and hand him the copy. Then he gives me a look I've never seen before. Something between surprise and irritation and gratitude. Who knows what's going on there. Whatever it is, his reaction makes me tense up enough that the stapler unleashes its wrath on me.

"Ow!!"

"Stay still." He calmly removes the staple from my finger.

The sight of blood always makes me queasy, which is beyond inconvenient when I'm an accident-prone nimrod. So Dad keeps me distracted, to discourage barfing.

"You okay?" he asks.

Funny ... he managed the words I couldn't use on him.

"It just stings," I reply.

Let me clarify here that "cool" is not a word I would automatically equate with my dad. It's not that he's square so much as just a little old-fashioned—like how he carries a handkerchief in his suit pocket. Something my grandpa had taught him: "gentlemen are always prepared." It's a bit of a lost art, since there are plenty of "guys," and lots of "dudes," and even more "losers." But "gentlemen" are a rarity, and whatever it takes to create them is what makes him silently wrap that handkerchief around my bleeding finger.

Then, without a word, he's gone. Will Sarazen, heading into another job interview. Into the abyss. Unaware of the gentleman that he is.

I study the white clump of cloth encircling my hand, contemplating, "What kind of dumbass staples their own finger?" and "How big of a man does it take to not call out that dumbass for being so dumb in the first place?"

Apparently, it takes a man like my dad. I learned something about him just now. That sometimes his silence isn't a bad thing. Sometimes, it's just the right amount of noise.

Huh. You think you know someone for fifteen years, and then one day you realize, there's like a whole new side of them you never saw before. A surprisingly cool side. And it creates this, sort of, warm and fuzzy bonding moment, that comes out of nowhere and saves my dumb ass a trip to the emergency room.

But we'll just keep that to ourselves, since my online version of the whole incident is way more elaborate and grotesque. I've already posted photos.

3

FAMOUS LAST WORDS

"You stop bleeding."

I'll wait. Just gonna let you go with this one.

Yes, that's how she phrased it. My grandma had a way with words. She was the only person I ever knew who could be charming and eloquent one minute, and cussing like a sailor the next. It often depended on her proximity to the liquor cabinet, but she typically found the right words for every situation.

I asked Grandma once, "How do you know when you're officially grown up?"

"You stop bleeding," she said.

For context, let me just add that I was like, eleven at the time, and had just seen that gross presentation in health class. So, naturally, I assumed she meant menopause. But then that barometer would effectively leave out half the population, so I pressed for more.

"Does that apply to everybody?"

Then she smiled, which would have been a kind of sweet moment ... if her dentures had been in. Seriously, other than gums and the discussion of blood, it might have been a Hallmark card. But once she slid her clackers in, she clammed up like a witness for the mob.

Maybe she didn't know what she meant, and was hoping that I'd work it out and get back to her. But that didn't happen. Grandma died last year.

She was my mom's mom. Losing her only added to the strain of the year, so I try to cut my mom some slack whenever she gets a little clingy and paranoid. I haven't really experienced much death. My grandpa died when I was little, so I don't remember a whole lot about that time. My other grandparents are still kicking down in Florida, tossing Ensure and rum into the blender. I did have a hamster named Petey that I found in a somewhat rigid yoga pose in his cage one day—which, frankly, had me envisioning dollar signs—until I processed that he forgot the cardinal rule to breathe. Other than that, the unraveling of the mortal coil is a pretty foreign concept to me.

But one thing I have noticed: everybody reacts to death differently, and no matter how many psychologists or experts try to tell you what to expect, there's no foolproof method to prepare for the end. Sure, you can leave instructions and buy prepaid plans with air pillows and watertight seals, but let's face it, there's only so much you can do ahead of time. Once it happens, it's a whole new ballgame, and how we respond is more of an "in the moment" kind of thing, rather than a solid plan. My mom is proof of that.

For months after Grandma died, Mom acted out by body-blocking me every time I tried to go out the door.

Now, this is aggravating enough when parents already do it as a habit. Just because you're a teenager who naturally feels invincible, they invariably feel they want to lock you away until you're thirty-five. But then when you toss in guilt and grief and mortality and a slew of other pent-up baggage, it's pretty hard to sidestep those good intentions without coming off as utterly cold and ruthless.

Of course, the traditional rationale is "Wait until you have kids, then you'll understand." Here's a newsflash, people: even if I were screwing around (I'm not ... like it's any of your business), I don't plan to have kids anytime soon. So the whole "you'll get it one day" angle doesn't fly right now. Considering that their parents used it on them—and they ignored it, too—it's a joke that any adult even bothers to try that line. But in moments of desperation, we're all forced to scrape the bottom of the argument barrel and just hope that our opponent is too dazzled by our footwork to notice the cheap shot.

Ultimately, we supposedly all turn into our parents one day. I personally haven't seen it yet, and am absolutely on board with keeping it that way. Not that I can't stomach my parents. Sure, they can be annoying at times, but for the most part, they're within cruising level on the tolerance radar. And compared to what some of my friends are dealing with, I got off easy. My parents, at least, don't *try* to be an endless hassle. But turning into them? That's the plan? Whatever happened to boundaries? Although their physical manifestations haven't hit the slippery slope yet—and given into the floral prints and socks with sandals that run rampant with my grandparents—it's an unspoken rule that such horrors are on the horizon, because once you make the risky fashion choice to stop looking in the mirror, the mental house of cards has already started to fall.

The thing with my parents is, every time I think I've figured them out, they manage to lose me again. Most kids would agree. Sometimes, there's a coded language, and if you focus enough, you can discern the hidden meaning. Kind of like baby sign language, for big people. But other times, they're just flat out baffling, and I'm in no mood to spend my entire youth trying to dissect the unknown. Plus, if my parents are the benchmark for what's to come, I'm only going to be confused again in adulthood. So why not just let me be my chaotic teenage self, and accept that I'll address any lingering issues later?

Unfortunately, it's the job of some adults to muddy that path with their own detours. In this case …

"Why would your guidance counselor need to see us?" Mom barked, clutching the note purposely printed on hot pink paper that subliminally screams "Look at me!"

… Or was that her screaming? I think I blacked out for a second.

"Um … beats me."

What a crock. I totally knew why. But I wasn't about to tell her that I forgot to go to Spanish class … for a week. I just had other things to do, and a girl can only juggle so much. Comprendé?

It wasn't like I left school grounds, so technically, it wasn't ditching. I was in the library, pretending to do a book report while secretly checking out the hot new transfer bad boy who somehow got assigned to fourth period in the bowels of study hall.

It was a fleeting—albeit mesmerizing—flirtation, until that hag, Tiffany-what's-her-name, wormed her tawdry little self into the middle of it. She's one of those girls my grandma used to call "Cloudy with a chance of anything." You know the type: the skank who consistently ruins your day, while making someone else's. I say throw 'em all onto their own island, and let it turn into *Lord of the Flies* with emery boards. Bon voyage, Be-atch.

I suspect that my guidance counselor was tortured by a Tiffany back in her day. But instead of taking the high road and moving on, she has since devoted her life to putting the kibosh on anyone who's having more fun than her. Which is basically everyone.

Normally, Mom would have been all over this one—talking to the counselor, finding out what makes me tick, and figuring out a rational defense to effectively lock me in my room while skirting the laws of child imprisonment. But much to Mom's dislike, karma has once again smiled upon me, burdening her with phase two of the Bridezilla interview: the obligatory "dog and pony show" at her floral shop. Canceling would have meant losing the account, and at this point, the prospect of a huge payday took precedence over her burning desire to mold me into a model citizen. So Dad drew the short straw as my legal representation.

"Can I drive?" I dared to ask.

I should have known this would tack extra years onto my pending sentence, but like a convict facing their last meal, I figured I might as well pig out. Mom didn't bite, even when I theorized that Dad was still in no condition to drive. Although, she must be keeping smelling salts next to the bed, because he does appear a tad more alert lately. Or maybe it's just a form of heightened awareness that comes up from time to time ... like dogs hearing sirens. God, what a maddening skill that would be. Picture it: you're just minding your own business, cleaning your crotch, when a piercing shrill comes out of nowhere because some knucklehead with opposable thumbs has done something ludicrous enough to warrant either the police or medical attention. Did you wish to have your peace and tranquility shattered? No. But there you go. Enjoy being you.

Come to think of it, that's where my dad's at right now. He was just living his life, crunching numbers, when his peace and tranquility went out the window, too. That's what happens with sirens. Man or beast, our natural tendency is to either cover our ears or howl. So when a siren goes off in your life, you've pretty much just got to wait on the side of the road until the thing passes ... and hope that nothing slams into you in the meantime.

"Out of character." "Subpar." "Disappointing."

Relax, we get it. No need to elaborate.

"We're concerned about this unusual behavior," she elaborates.

Way to go, Ginormous. Okay, even I admit I thought it was kinda cruel when I first heard that my guidance counselor, Mrs. Norman, was nicknamed "Ginormous" because she's basically, like, the size of a grizzly. Add to that her not-so-discreetly bleached mustache, and the inevitable Bigfoot comparison ensued. The rumors of her existence were legendary, but I initially wondered, "Could she really be that much of a Sasquatch?"

I underestimated.

I guess it's nothing that some heavy makeup, an epilator and a large pair of binding sandals wouldn't cure. But since none of those alternatives have been put to good use, the result is something of an anthropological car crash that's impossible to look away from.

Dad's staring at her like she's an alien with three heads. In light of the crap hand dealt to him lately, I thought he might take the sympathetic route and not look at her like a pod person with overactive testosterone. No such luck, chick. Obviously, Dad's people skills are worn down. Ginormous keeps fishing for a response, having no inkling what she's up against.

"We feel that Greer—"

I raise my hand.

"Yes?" she asks.

"From now on, I'd like to be called 'Reger.'"

That puts a cork in her. Unfortunately, it uncorks Dad.

"This again?"

I forge ahead. "R-e-g-e-r. I'd like it entered into the record, please."

Ginormous opens my file, the classic slap of intimidation. Few things in life are as unnerving as files. Who knows what's in them, or who's seen them. When somebody has a file on you, it doesn't bode well. Even if there are good things inside—commendations, letters of reference—there's always the potential for one deep, dark piece of personal eccentricity to upend the whole thing.

Something we do that *we* may embrace as completely normal and acceptable, but isn't viewed with such love through the status quo lens. Case in point ...

"Your file says your name is Greer," she drearily points out.

"I take no responsibility for that."

Dad gives me a sour look, probably reconsidering my inheritance.

"'Reger' is not a name," he admonishes.

"Well, I only have five letters. There's not much to work with, is there?"

Ginormous makes some condescending grunt and jots notes into my file. Even Dad picks up on the hairiness of that one. Yeah, I punned.

"Look, this is not an issue, all right?" he protests. "It's just attitude."

An elitist sniff. Then more jotting.

"And what exactly has spurred this attitude?" Ginormous smugly probes.

"She's fifteen," Dad shrugs. "Where should I begin?"

Oh no, more dissecting to come. I quickly look for an escape route, realizing that the drab, puke green brick walls would afford little or no climbing traction. I debate stuffing myself into the wastebasket, on the off chance that a charitable janitor will soon swing by, when Dad pops the unruly beast with a tranquilizer.

"Can we move on, please?"

I'm hoping this feeding frenzy is almost over, but it appears Ginormous isn't done savoring the kill.

"We're here to talk about Greer's lack of commitment to her studies," she says.

Sorry, lady. I can't let this one go.

"*Reger*. R-e-g-e-r. Clearly, I'm decent at spelling."

"That's enough!" Dad snaps.

It suddenly dawns on me that I'm sharing this wild kingdom with a closet crazy and a ticked off grizzly. Maybe it's time to shut up.

Ginormous takes her cue and proceeds to offer the proverbial laundry list of things I've allegedly done wrong, peppering the whole mix with words like "undisciplined," "slacking," and "uninspired."

Hmmm ... let's examine the evidence.

"Undisciplined?" With respect to my devout and absolute commitment to getting my driver's license as quickly as humanly possible, I would take issue with that one.

"Slacking?" Compared to every other teenager on the planet ... I'd say, "not so much."

"Uninspired?" Totally.

"To carry on with this behavior could jeopardize her future," Ginormous contends.

Dad sits silently, staring at her with such glazed eyes, you'd swear he just rolled out of a medical marijuana place. Then, miraculously, he somehow forms words.

"In what way?" Dad ponders.

"Excuse me?"

"You say she's jeopardizing her future. I'd like to know in what way."

Whoa. I can't see my face in the reflection of the cheap office furnishings, but right now I'm pretty sure I must look more dumfounded than a hillbilly at a spelling bee. What the hell is he talking about?

"She's sacrificing her academic standing," Ginormous responds, waiting for a gasp of horror from Dad. Nothing. So she plows ahead. "Which will undoubtedly limit her prospects for college, and a future career."

Still no response, until—

"So what's your solution?" Dad asks.

"Greer has to try harder," Ginormous surmises.

Another long, stoned silence. Did Dad secretly light up on the ride over here? And if so, how did I miss the party? Finally, he speaks.

"Why?"

Although I heartily applaud his train of thought, I have no clue as to how he got on board.

Much to her dismay, neither does Ginormous. Now she's looking at me to make sense of all this, and offer answers. Some pearl of wisdom to decipher my father's incoherent ramblings. A minute ago I was useless. Now the Queen of Beasts needs me to be her Sherpa, guiding her up the treacherous slope of this conversation, to bring her desperate soul to the peak of illumination.

Don't look at me, lady. I gave up a long time ago.

"I beg your pardon?" Ginormous retorts.

"Why should she try harder?" Dad questions. "To go to college? To get a degree? To get a good job?"

"Yes, yes, and yes," in this Ginormous world.

"And then what?"

"I don't understand."

"No, you don't," Dad insists.

I have no idea where this is going, but I'm thoroughly fascinated.

"You tell kids if they work hard and pay their dues,

they'll be rewarded in the real world," Dad begins. "Have you looked outside lately? Turned on the television? Read the news? The real world doesn't care anymore. It doesn't care about me. It doesn't care that I gave twenty years to a job I was damn good at and had pulled out from under me. It doesn't care that I got good grades and have a family to support. It doesn't care that people like me get up every day, wondering if this is going to be the day that changes our lives. Because the real world will still exist tomorrow, in whatever form it's going to be. But the rest of us have to exist as a by-product of that world, whether we like it or not. And that world doesn't care. So don't sit here and lie to these kids, and tell them that your way is the only way. I followed your way. I did everything I was supposed to do. I went out into the real world, and it crashed down around me. So what kind of 'guidance' do you have to offer me? What advice do you have for me now, that I can tell my daughter when this potentially happens to her? Huh?"

Wow. This crackpot tour was pleasantly worth the price of admission. All these months we thought Dad was losing his mind. Who knew that, instead, he was tapping into a well of controlled anger that was about to erupt all over the establishment? I love it. Ginormous just got her ass handed to her—which is not only some heavy lifting, but also a pretty clunky maneuver, given her dimensions.

He's *so* my hero right now.

4

LAST DITCH ATTEMPT

"Devoted Father." "Loving Wife." "Dear Friend." Those are the words they use when you're gone.

"Out of character." "Subpar." "Disappointing." That's what you get when you're still around.

Something about certain words can hover in the air when you hear them, like a foul odor. Their permanence is in your head, whether they're true or not. Other words are carved in stone. Literally. I know, because I'm looking at them. And while we're on the subject … who knew there were so many types of granite? I'm all for variety, but it's a bit much.

Sorry, rewind …

There's this cemetery along the drive to school. It's pretty old and creepy, just by nature of being a cemetery. Dead people go in and don't come out. I hope not, at any rate. Living things—like flowers—go in and sometimes die there. The grass is continuously getting cut, so even things that have a shot at survival can only thrive so much. And considering that most of us will likely end up in one of these places, cemeteries are a good incentive to live it up now, because the odds are not in our favor.

Until now, my only interaction with this place has been on a pendulum somewhere between avoidance and intrigue. I almost got suckered into coming here last Halloween, when my tiresome uber doofus of a neighbor, Snyder, hung a pair of deathly pimped-out mannequins from one of the trees, in a lame effort to terrorize a group of unsuspecting freshmen. If Snyder had put a little more thought into his grand scheme, it might have worked better. But once his eagle-eyed manager from the mall spotted the missing decor while visiting the remains of his Aunt Agnes, the jig was up pretty quick. Typical Snyder, constantly barking up the wrong tree.

Mistakenly stuck in complacent disregard, I thought I'd just carry on being creeped out from a safe distance and avoid this place until absolutely necessary. But alas, here we are, enjoying the scenery at "Atrophy's Acres." No, that's not the real name. I'm a teenager. I can't bother with details, so I just make stuff up as I go along.

Trust me, if I had been driving, this never would have happened. But with Dad at the wheel, the mere glimpse of a "HELP WANTED" sign on the gate was enough to send the car thrusting into reverse, barreling through the entrance, past the "Isle of Doves," around the hairpin curve at the "Garden of Eternal Rest," dodging a squirrel heading toward the mausoleum with no name, near the fountain that spits like Bellagio's bastard child, just to end up in front of the Main Office, where Dad now stands frozen in a fit of nerves.

I would say "Just kill me now," but under the circumstances, it could prove a tad too convenient.

"Explain to me again why we're here?" I ask.

Dad stands there, looking at the office windows like the gates of purgatory. Time to be judged. He sighs. I tell myself that he's probably just exhausted from his verbal dance with Ginormous. She's quite a hunk o' carnivore, after all. But then Dad says something I haven't heard from him before.

"I need a job."

No shouting. No mumbling. No noticeable inflection. Just the words, straight out of his mouth and into the air, hovering with their own stench ... and by definition, carved in stone.

As for me, things aren't that concise.

"*Here??*" I blurt out, horrified. "There's probably a mini-mart down the street that's hiring. You could sell nachos and cigarettes, and just work with the soon-to-be dead, not the *dead* dead. That could be fun, huh?"

Dad's not on board, which becomes glaringly apparent when he drops a little bombshell about how he used to work part-time as a cemetery groundskeeper, when he was in college.

"It wasn't so bad," Dad recalls. "Kind of peaceful, really."

How marvelous to dig up those bothersome skills now. I start to protest further, until we hear—

"Are you the Footes?"

It just so happens that the Owner-Mortician type who runs the place has emerged from his haunted mansion to troll for wandering clients.

"The Foote family? Four o'clock appointment?"

Oh no. A foreboding sales pitch was not on my daily agenda. But since this guy kinda reminds me of my cousin's dog, Digby—friendly enough, although a little too obsessed with burying things—I'll keep calling him that to comfort myself, rather than scream in terror at the top of my lungs. Meanwhile, Dad again appears zoned to the gills. Seriously, must I do everything?

"Um, no," I say. "We're not Feete."

"Oh, I'm so sorry," Digby apologizes. "I just saw you lingering ..."

This may be a total aside, but "linger" is one of those words that just never has a good connotation, no matter the context. Stalkers "linger." Bad tastes "linger." Smells "linger." There was even a kid in my science class who never seemed to bathe, and fittingly got the nickname "Linger." He left an impression wherever he went, even after he'd left the room. Speaking of which, can we go now?

"I'm here to apply for the job," Dad declares.

Tell me he did not just say that! Frick, where is the zombie version of Dad when I need him?

"Which job, specifically?" Digby perks up.

Oh, goody, you mean there's more than one? Marvelous. Months and months of Dad scouring the internet for anything even remotely available in his field, with sadly slim pickings. All the while, "Death's Door" is on a hiring binge.

"Anything you have," Dad says, without a blink.

Turns out, the list is quite enchanting: "Gravedigger" or "Gravedigger."

Long story short, there was a tag-team of brothers—
the Zimonovich twins—who used to plant the customers
... until they got deported. The twins, that is, not the
customers. Digby isn't elaborating on the technicalities of
immigration, but apparently, it had something to do with
vodka and a shaky definition of a "harem."

Dad quickly discourages any further details, afraid that
my adolescent ears will be forever scathed. Little does he
know that despite his chivalry, I've been routinely
subjected to murder, mayhem, and debauchery on any
random night of television. But how sweet of him to care.

As for the job, Dad mulls over the upsides.

It's physical work, so no more guilt about not going to
the gym. Chalk this up as **Positive Point #1.**

It's a reason to get dressed and go outside, preventing
anymore potentially awkward glimpses up a loose
bathrobe, while feebly attempting Pilates in front of
daytime TV. For all concerned, this will gratefully be
christened **Positive Point #2.**

Small fortune that will be saved on family therapy after
too many inadvertent glimpses up loose bathrobe. On
behalf of Mom, Liv, myself and the dog, the
aforementioned shall be known as **Positive Points #3, 4,
5 and 6.**

Considering that Dad's Unemployment Insurance is
on its last breath, there's not much time to spare. A
gambling man might roll the dice and ride the
government wave a bit longer. But Dad dealt with
numbers for a living, so he knows the drill.

"Can I get an application?" he inquires, as my mouth
hangs open.

This brings us to **Point #7**, which may be viewed as equally positive and negative, depending on the circumstance.

Positive: Dad's skill sets could now list the charming enhancement of "gravedigging."

Negative: Mom will likely collapse in a fit of hysteria, upon hearing of his new career path.

Positive: Upon collapsing, there could now be a freshly dug hole to catch her.

Negative: It's not the type of place you want to be, until necessary.

In highbrow terms, this is what's known as a "quandary." In everyday life, it's known as "sucks to be you." Whether Dad consciously acknowledged that fact while filling out the application, I'll never know. Digby must have seen something I didn't, but whatever happened, it was enough to make him interview Dad on the spot, and offer him the job.

Oh, and the other family eventually did show up. I watched them pass, one Foote in front of the other. Like the entire day, it was a strange parade.

I can't get a break. Just when I think I've got possibly *the* biggest bombshell to drop when we get home—that Dad's career plans have rapidly gone south—another colossal bombshell is circling the air, ready to crash land at any moment.

"Are you serious??" I stammer.

"What? You think I'd *joke* about this??"

Here we go. It's so exhausting being the sane sibling.

"Well, you are kinda smiling," I inform Liv. "Or is that a grimace?"

More like indigestion. Brought on by heightened nerves, and possible morning sickness. You guessed it ... she's stopped bleeding.

"Have you taken a test?" I stupidly ask.

"Sort of," she waffles.

"What does that mean?"

"I peed on it. But then I got nervous and dropped it in the toilet and couldn't tell what it said."

"Then get another one," I say, because "Duh" feels a touch too smug.

"*Duh*. I did."

She slaps the pregnancy kit onto the bathroom counter.

"And?" I probe.

"I haven't taken it yet. Oh, but I picked up some Monistat, too, just in case that's it, and I'm wigging for no reason. I mean, I know something's off, so it's got to be one of the two, right?"

I don't have the heart to burst her delusional bubble. Not that either scenario is appealing, but at least a yeast infection doesn't take eighteen years to go away.

NOW A QUICK WORD FROM OUR SPONSORS: *"Ever have that 'something's off' feeling? Now you can get answers in one easy step. Simply urinate on a stick. You'll have results in no time. Side effects may include vomiting, dizziness, hysterical blindness, profuse sweating and an overall loss of sensation. Consult your doctor for denial lasting more than four hours. Beer and pork*

rinds will not protect you from STDs or pregnancy when the male persuasion gives them priority over the 'love glove.' Do not take pregnancy tests while consuming alcohol or operating heavy machinery, as this may result in the urge to bash nearby objects over your loser boyfriend's head. Proceed responsibly."
WE NOW RETURN TO OUR PROGRAM.

"I don't need this right now!" Liv rails. "I'm only halfway through college. I haven't even gone through my 'gay' phase yet!"

"Is that required??"

"It's elective, but still …"

Running out of patience, I hold out the pregnancy kit. Liv huffs and closes the bathroom door. I wait outside, trying not to be a snob, since I want no ticket to any trip involving diapers and anal thermometers. But I'm willing to be supportive in this moment, while keeping a safe distance when the door opens. Look, we all make half-baked decisions from time to time. Some are simple fixes, but others are so monumentally boneheaded they belong in the "Lamebrain Hall of Fame." This would qualify as the latter.

To be fair, Liv's not dumb by nature. Just impulsive. Which means she got caught up in the moment. This setting could sound romantic, except for the ill-timed detail that Liv has a tendency to forget her birth control pills, since she's never been big on schedules. As for her dud of a boyfriend, he was way too drunk to properly prepare for their night of wild romance. The pork rinds somehow got purchased, but "the little rubber thing designed to spare you a lifetime of unexpected commitment and hemorrhaging finances" didn't manage to make the shopping list. In effect, they both ignored their back-up plans. So here we are.

Now Mom and Dad are having it out in the living room, since he's obviously broken the news about his new job. I'm massively bummed I'm missing the whole thing. Just the chance of Dad doing anything on a whim is virtually unfathomable, so Mom's ordinary level of whinging has traveled to a whole new stratosphere, which—although terrifying—would be fascinating to see. Trust me, if Liv wasn't determining her fate with a pee stick, she'd absolutely be on board, too. Instead, I have to settle for eavesdropping on piercing shrills and garbled responses that may or may not be English, since I promised Liv that I wouldn't abandon her for five minutes, or however long these things take.

I can't tell if Mom is mad, or if the guttural growls and hyperventilating are involuntary reflexes. There's definitely shrieking, but not the "Yay! I won the lottery!" version of shrieking. This is more like an opera singer sucking helium: loud, freakish, and not easy on the ears. Considering that Mom has been nudging Dad for months to get a job—*any* job—that would help make ends meet, you'd think she'd be thrilled. But the idea of shovels and grave liners has her a bit skeeved out. Join the club, lady.

It's not like Dad has any serial-killer tendencies—at least, I'll keep telling myself that. Yet, there has to be very little comfort in the thought that statistics say you're most likely to be murdered by your spouse. So the fact that your spouse is now going to be trained in the proper disposal of bodies isn't exactly a cause for celebration.

Liv pokes her head out of the bathroom, shoving the piss meter my way.

"What is that?"

Repulsed, I take a quick glance. "Looks like a plus sign."

"Are you sure? 'Cuz it could be a minus with a discoloration mark. Look again."

"No, it's a plus sign."

"Yeah, but this kit was made in Canada," Liv reasons. "Maybe in one of those French-speaking districts. You know what that means …"

"That neither of us understands you?"

"No, the French have that whole metric thing. Which means their math is different. So a plus sign might really mean minus. Eh?"

Now she's just embarrassing herself. Lying is one thing, but going along with sheer lunacy is another. I can't sink that low, even in her moment of need. Some people just have to be pummeled with the truth.

"I'd bet a plus sign would still be a plus sign," I hold firm.

Liv stares at me, knowing full well she's treading on thin ice in the logic department. But, still, she clings to idiocy.

"Well, let's just see about that," she snipes.

Two hours, and nearly every Googled page later, Liv begrudgingly concedes that there is no wonky math to explain away her test. She's knocked up, and has sworn me to total secrecy until she can find just the right moment to break the news to our parents. We both agree that now is probably not the best time. And since I missed the floorshow tonight, I don't need to get screwed again. Liv has proven how well that can work out.

So, let's recap:

I got an academic tongue lashing from a badly-dressed wildebeest.

Liv's gonna pop out a kid.

Mom's on the verge of a nervous breakdown.

And Dad's a gravedigger.

... And how was *your* day??

5

LAST I HEARD

"Beware the Steaming Buddha."

If only they were mere words. If only they were an exaggeration. They are neither.

Oh, I'm sorry … am I sounding too "drama queen" for you? Then allow me to stuff you into the quaking boots from where I'm standing, so you can get a clear perspective. Watch and learn, people.

It's like this …

TV has that Emergency Broadcast System. Civil defense has air raid sirens. Broadway has the *Times* review. And like it or not, teenagers have their own warning system to prepare for impending disaster.

It's called "texting." Yes, I know it's not safe to do from behind the wheel. I get that. But before we take the wheel, we must brace ourselves. We must be prepared. We must be warned: "Beware the Steaming Buddha."

The sending of these four words has served to give a screaming heads-up to countless oblivious souls who venture into Driver's Ed class, without the faintest hint of the dungpile they're about to step in. Trust me, the sheer prospect of spending an hour in the shadow of the Buddha is far more daunting than the tightest three-point turn. And as if that weren't enough—he's also *steaming!!*

No, not "steaming" like a total hottie. I wish. "Steaming" like a fat teapot.

I don't get the physics of it all, but supposedly it has something to do with condensation and evaporation. That's what the smart kid said, anyway. Personally, I'd conclude that it relates more to the Buddha taking a shine to one too many cheeseburgers in his day, and there's only so much insulation a body needs before it has to sweat some off.

Alas, the villagers huddle together, sharing stories of the legend. One by one, they recount the horror of coming face to belly with "The Steaming Buddha"—a.k.a. Herb Kleinwalder. Oh yeah, he has a real name. Even *the* Buddha had a real name … I think. Did I mention that I tend to doze in History? But I feel fairly confident in going out on the limb that says—like the Dalai Lama— Buddha, himself, had a "real-person" name at some point. Otherwise, his birth certificate would have just said "Buddha" and been kicked back by some jaded County Clerk in no mood for spiritual humor. And—correct me if I'm wrong here—unlike this version, the real Buddha didn't steam. He was more about enlightenment. Not freaking out innocent children.

While a label like "The Steaming Buddha" would make an epic name for a Chinese restaurant—whose fortune cookies would skirt the pleasantries with messages like "You're a loser, suck it up"—the fact that anyone deserves the title in the first place is simply one more sign of society's impending collapse. You gotta admit, there's a twisted fascination with observing that percentage of humanity that's largely gone off a mental cliff. In this case, with the girth involved, you could almost call it a "mass exodus."

Now, there's no real consensus of precisely when young Herbie's psychological burrito dropped a few beans, but his official morphing into a Buddha is suspected to have occurred around his late twenties. Conventional wisdom holds that the moment of epiphany was when he couldn't fit into his yoga tights anymore. So Herb decided that even if his body wasn't illuminated, his mind was on a roll ... specifically, a cinnamon roll that was calling to him from the bakery across the street. A resulting overdose of sugar compelled him to want to steer a path for young minds, but the whole clarity thing hadn't kicked in enough to make him reach beyond the literal boundaries of that plan.

So we ended up here, in a car the size of a washing machine—which, by proximity to "Le Buddha Esteamed," has become something of a mobile sauna. Trust me when I say curly hair is NOT a good look for me, so this is not a place that either of us wants to be. To sum up, I can't describe my inner joy, because at this moment, I have none. Could this nightmare get any worse?

"So, Greer," the Buddha begins.

Okay, I'm gonna stop asking if things can get worse, because that just opens the door for the universe to prove they can.

"Call me 'Reger," I maintain.

"Pardon?"

"Reger. R-e-g-e-r."

Buddha checks his clipboard.

"Reger? Is that a name?"

"For now."

He starts to scribble. "Is it short for something?"

I mull it over. "Regurgitate?"

As if by magic, the Buddha stops steaming. The mere possibility that any parent would name their kid such a thing has made his blood run cold.

"Your full name is *'Regurgitate'?*" he asks, aghast.

"Not legally. But the whole thing does make me want to heave."

"I'm not following you," the Buddha fesses up, which I gotta say, is fairly disappointing, given that Buddhas are expected to comprehend things that the average person can't grasp. Or at least that's the marketing angle.

So I lay out my case, complete with unscientific facts and polls that support the position that everybody needs a flexible name. Otherwise, you're just stuck in name limbo and are, therefore, immediately less interesting.

"A person's value is not measured in a name," he advises. "It's measured from within."

"Yeah, but my insides aren't happy with Greer, either," I argue.

"So you made an anagram out of it?"

"Um ... sure?" I have no idea what we're talking about.

For a moment, it looks like I may get away with this one; that maybe the Steaming Buddha will be the one person who actually *is* tolerant enough to accept someone without overly analyzing every motive. That is, until ...

"Your aura is not a 'Reger,'" he obstinately says. "What about your middle name? Anything to work with there?"

"Nora," I answer. "Four letters."

"'Nora' is a lovely name. Why not use that?"

Once again, the whole flexibility argument is getting lost in translation. Even though I don't speak Buddhese, that shouldn't be a prerequisite, since my stance is pretty clear. I just want options, damnit. I plead my case once more, fighting a raging temptation to spew profanity, since Buddha's acting a tad prude.

I can almost hear the wheels whirring in his head, mulling the bountiful harvest of letters that destiny has so graciously afforded me in the name department.

"Aron," he offers up. "Just reverse it. A-r-o-n. A male spelling, but still ..."

Oh, right. Like my life isn't complicated enough. Please, let's make it more of a puzzle. Perhaps the look on my face has riled him, because it seems there's a shelf life to Buddha's whole "serenity" thing.

"What?" he spouts. "You think 'Reger' is gonna win beauty pageants?"

Contrary to popular belief, "subtlety" is not automatically part of the Buddha handbook. This steaming chubbo knows how to cut to the core ... and open a few pores along the way. So the good news is you get a mini-facial while dodging barbs. The bad news is that the name-calling isn't confined to just the car. At least, not just ours.

"Hey, Crypt Keeper!"

And so it begins. Another day of juvenile heckling from the world's jackass brigade. Their head comrade would be Donny Presder, better known as "Pester." I would call him a pea-brain, but that would be an insult to peas, which are certainly higher functioning.

Pester slings his snarky arrows from a car across the street, as he and his minions giggle.

"Shouldn't you be driving a hearse?" he spits.

Really? As if being a sophomore isn't debilitating enough, now I've also gotta endure "shade by association?" I'm frankly astonished that Pester even noticed me, since he rarely puts his phone down long enough to actually look where he's going.

"Friend of yours?" the Buddha wonders.

"Not in this life, or any other," I huff.

"Now, Greer—"

"Reger ..."

"You must remember that everyone in this life is your brother," the Buddha pontificates.

"But I don't have a brother," I point out. "Just a sister with a bun in the oven."

"The miracle of life should not be minimized," the Buddha scolds.

"Oh, it's not minimal," I assure. "Believe me, she's measuring her ass every day."

The Buddha starts steaming again, evidently not amused.

"Sorry," I shrink. "I meant to say 'nether regions.'"

True to his name, Pester can't let it go, lobbing more ridicule from afar.

"Don't drive into a ditch! You could hit your old man!"

"Oh that's genius!" I yell in return. "You spend all night comin' up with that one? Turdhead!"

"Reger," the Buddha interjects, "Don't engage. This is a key lesson when behind the wheel."

"Hey, it's not like I'm texting! Yelling is still legal, isn't it?"

"Do not encourage angry confrontations with other drivers. Road rage can kill."

"So can stress, if you don't let it out!" I surmise.

"Just take a breath," the Buddha guides. "In ... and out."

Oh God, now he's demonstrating.

"Innnnnn ... and oouuuuuuutt."

As much as I had been warned about the oddities of the Steaming Buddha, even I didn't see this one coming. Most times, his peculiarity was limited to his own actions, not celebrated as a group effort.

"C'mon, now. Do it with me. Innnn ... and ouuuttt."

I play along just for show, and because I don't want to be docked points that could delay my ticket to freedom through a driver's license. I spot Pester and his toads watching from a safe distance, warily evaluating the self-analysis now running rampant throughout the sauna on wheels.

From what I've heard, yogis teach acceptance—an embrace of the unexpected. Fine, I can deal. I can even begin to feel the unfurling of my inner lotus flower ... in the form of at least one appendage. I slowly, discreetly, flip off Pester, violating all the rules of Zen. Sure, it's not the high road, but right now, it's more important to salvage my reputation.

See, I do pride myself on being at least somewhat clued in to the cultural pulse, even when it bores me to tears. Not that I want to go mainstream with the other lemmings, but being aware of the behavioral norm is key if you want to come out of your teen years intact ... according to Liv, at any rate. But now that she's launching into a new orbit on the baby rocket, it might be wise to hitch my "insight wagon" to another star. At any rate, I know this much: even if you aren't the *coolest* kid in school, it's absolutely crucial to NOT be the most *uncool*. For all but a precious few, this can be a daily balancing act. On the typical hierarchy of cool, one person is on the mountaintop, and one person is underwater. The rest of us live somewhere in-between ... and occasionally, have to tunnel out.

As a result, we sometimes have to defend ourselves from the slings and arrows of those pricks who deem themselves higher on the social spectrum. So I flash my finger like a lightsaber, daring Pester to come at me with more. I'd bet even the dimmest of guys has heard the rumor about hell's fury and a woman scorned. I can promise that scenario is nothing compared to a teenager having a bad hair day while being psychoanalyzed by a mondo human vaporizer with a need to share. Pester's a blithering moron, but his goons at least manage to see the warning signs. He and his dunce party peel off into the sunset.

Wow ... this Zen thing is for real. I'm feeling more centered already.

*

I take back what I just said.

As if not having your driver's license is not already a big enough drag, I forgot about the obligatory walk of shame after Driver's Ed. To describe it as painful doesn't even begin to cover it. Your backpack feels tons heavier, weighted down with the crushing burden of not yet being vehicularly mobile. Your spirit is frayed like a piñata at a bully's birthday party. And your mind wanders like a disoriented soul crawling across the never-ending desert of material denial.

Today is more disturbingly vivid than usual, with Pester and the Steaming Buddha playing volleyball in my head. Between insufferable blabbermouths and unsolicited advice, I can't decide which is more annoying. It's not that I think I'm always right—I just generally know that I am. So to have outside forces continually trying to sway that opinion is beyond irritating.

The more I dwell on my time with the Buddha, the more frazzled I get. Not just because he's something of a head case to begin with, but also because he has this habit of tapping into stuff that I don't particularly feel like tapping. Not in a gross, "creepy stranger" kind of way, but in an "Oh no, you didn't" kind of way. For better or worse, he brings up things I never really thought about, which can only mean the world wanted me to ignore them in the first place. But then, all teachers do that. It's like they're not happy unless they're "challenging" us with concepts that they're convinced we'll never figure out otherwise. Give it time, I say, and let the world teach us by example. Otherwise, you're just gonna piss me off, and—like the Steaming Buddha—create a monster head case, with frizz. Which makes me contemplate …

"Why don't I carry a hat?"

I know, I know … my mind is veering off track, considering I've never been a hat person. But just stop and contemplate hats for a second. Some people are born for the look. Am I right? While, others—though they try—just can't pull off the style.

Truth is, I've never acquired a taste for headwear. My only explanation is that I was emotionally scarred when learning to rollerblade and being forced to wear the obligatory helmet. After an especially sweaty outing on an August afternoon, I ran into—or rather, *crashed* into—my seventh grade crush, Rocky Tellerado.

Now, you gotta understand the significance of this encounter to appreciate the depth of my enduring despair. Not only did he have the most breathtaking name known to man (I dare you to say it aloud and not get a little excited), but he was one of those guys who made everything look so easy. Walking, talking, breathing … whatever, he had it down. Like he never had to work to be amazing, it just happened. And I'm tellin' you, if anybody could pull off a hat, he could. I get weepy just thinking about his crushed blue baseball cap. Even in the tattered aftermath of the accident, it was a stunning fashion statement.

Which leads me to another reason to cry. Long story short, our collision sent my helmet askew, which meant I had to remove it in his presence. I'll never know if it was the pasted-down horror of helmet hair or the cratering wound over my eye that sufficiently put him off, but something went awry that day, and Rocky headed for the hills. He and his family moved that next spring, because I can only imagine that he begged to be busted out from the vicinity of lesser mortals who dared try to invade his magical airspace. Others might have found this maneuver pretentious, but such an Adonis couldn't be expected to wade in the muck of the masses. He deserved better, damnit. If he had stayed in the confines of our minor hemisphere, he, too, would have been subjected to the likes of the Steaming Buddha ... and why even attempt to mess with perfection?

I confess I never knew Rocky all that well. So it could be one big hormonal fantasy that, even at twelve, he was a giant among men. But I'll take that risk. I sometimes try to picture what he'd look like today, if the past three and a half years have been kind to him, or made him a hot mess. Either way, I'm sure he's dating up a storm, breaking hearts right and left, and probably graduated to felt fedoras by now.

Whoa ... gimme a sec. I need to come down.

Dang it! Why do I continually torture myself over this? He's probably turned into an arrogant dick. He may have been one all along, and I was too blinded by his sheer beauty to ever notice. That's what I'll keep telling myself, anyway, to lessen the bitter sting of loss. Either that, or this walk home is going to be absolutely endless, since I forgot to charge my iPod. If I can't fill my head with music, then all I'm gonna hear are the Buddha's ramblings ... over and over and over.

You see, after Pester and his henchmen fled the scene, the Buddha was more steamed than ever, wondering what was so pressing that it could possibly disrupt his fascinating discourse on left-hand turns. So I was forced to divulge how my Dad is now the local gravedigger … or, one of however many we have, since I've never bothered counting. I thought this would put a cork in the Buddha, and mercifully end the discussion. But, *nooooooo*.

"So you see it as a bad thing, what your Dad does?" he asked.

"Well, I wouldn't call it a conversation starter."

"So you think he just digs holes?"

Can you see where this is going? I was digging a hole for myself, because no matter what I said, the Steaming Buddha felt my response was unwarranted. Believe me, I tried everything.

The Diplomatic Approach: "He digs holes, yes … but to industry specifications."

"What else?" the Buddha probed.

Humor: "He digs up dirt on people?"

No laugh to be had. Buddha's sense of humor must have been thrown out with his skinny jeans.

Optimism: "He lays foundations for new homes?"

"And?" the Buddha badgered.

For crying out loud, pick one already.

Abstract: "He lines the walls with plastic? Which is … technically recycling?"

The Buddha wasn't buying anything I had to sell. So, inevitably we moved to …

Defeat: "Can you just tell me what I should think? Because I'm running out of options."

The Steaming Buddha mellowed to a simmer, relishing the chance to open a young mind.

"Your dad gives people their final resting place," he concluded. "The last material gift they get on this earth."

"Huh?" I gaped, horrified. "I thought Buddhas weren't into the whole 'materialism' thing?"

"Your father is a Buddhist?"

"No, you—"

Whoa ... I realized at that moment that the Steaming Buddha didn't know his nickname. How is that possible? All these years, no student ever blurted it out in a moment of blind panic while making a U-turn? He never heard any whispers among the gossipy sewing circle of the teacher's lounge? He's a rotund, mantra-spewing steam machine, for cryin' out loud. Did the idea never register that the inherent cruelty of teenagers was bound to make a mockery of that sooner or later?

"I what?" he countered.

Given that I was sitting within striking distance and strapped in by a seat belt that may or may not release for a fast getaway, I opted for self-preservation.

"You ... have a point," I said.

I wasn't about to be the human sacrifice who uttered his nickname to his face. My acne was finally clearing up, and I was within sight of a driver's license. If my fate was about to hit the fan, I was gonna go down swinging.

"Thank you for bringing it to my attention ... Mr. Kleinwalder."

I felt a snicker building in the base of my throat, and quickly passed it off as a cough. Damn you, sarcasm, you selfish muse.

He stared at me again, not sure if I was playing him. But thankfully the mercy gene kicked in just in time, and the Buddha retreated to his happy place, where he anxiously goes to escape the fact that slackers like me will be caring for him in his old age. Who knows, maybe that's the incentive for not dieting. The Buddha's hatched his own backup plan with junk food as a poison pill, for when society ultimately implodes.

Or maybe he just chose to embrace the cupcakes and live high on the hog. Regardless, the Buddha's steam cleaning his own personal path to nirvana, stopping at every conceivable drive-thru along the way. I gotta give props, 'cuz that's some serious dedication. I wonder if he was ever called "uninspired" by a Bigfoot in his day?

Oh goody, now Ginormous has been thrown into my cerebral mix. My brain hurts from massive overcrowding. To top it off, I accidentally missed my usual detour two blocks over, which lets me avoid the very spot where I am right now ... at the gates of the cemetery. Yep, *that* cemetery, where the paternal seed of my existence is flipping dirt patties as we speak.

Full disclosure, the detour is no bargain either, requiring me to cut through the parking lot of a Bingo hall. Every Thursday, there's the same group of cranky blue-hairs who pile out of a station wagon that looks like a lumberyard on wheels. From pictures I've seen, paneling was big in the '70s. But what on earth could those people have been smoking to ever think it belonged on car doors? And don't even get me started on the macramé seat covers. Life is simply too short to go there.

So here I stand, gazing through the wrought-iron

fence that separates the living from the dead, and the driver's license deficient from her shovel-wielding father. I don't readily recall Dad ever doing much gardening, but then again, I never paid much attention. I know he mowed the lawn, and would let me jump into piles of leaves. Which goes back to that secretly "cool" side of Dad that shows up from time to time.

But now I am paying attention, since Dad is digging deep inside—in more ways than one—and I'm on the outside, looking in. Wait, crap! Did he see me?

"Ow!!"

Oh crap!! Did he hear me??

I slowly peek up over a hedge, literally ready to meet my maker, when I confirm … he's still shoveling. Didn't see or hear a thing. Quick flashes and moaning must be commonplace here. That's handy, since I'm totally ready to leave—especially now that the psychobabble broken record of "The Steaming Buddha's Greatest Hits" starts spinning in my head. Track one: *"So you think he just digs holes?"*

I gotta bust out before I get spotted. But hold up … what if he did hear me? And see me? And what if he knows I'm watching? Maybe it's just as hard for him to stomach that wrought-iron divide between us as it is for me to stand on this side of the fence. What if he wishes that he could make a pile of leaves for both of us to jump into, to go back to days that weren't so perturbing?

Whoa, I definitely have to change my mental tune, because if I start hearing the Buddha pontificating about the nuances of time travel, I'm gonna have to hurt someone. Even scarier than that, is the other voice ringing in my ears—that buffoon Pester, who has now annihilated my theory of using "Reger" as an alternate name, since the cat-calls of "Reger Mortis" are bound to follow.

Time to go. C'mon feet, feel free to get moving. Please, or I might start watching again.

Like I'm doing now. Watching. *Really* watching ... because around another hedge, is a coffin. And then I notice the people, in dark suits and black dresses. And the limo parked along the road. I've been so caught up in watching Dad, I didn't notice the funeral that just ended. Some of the mourners are still hanging out nearby. I don't get it. They could leave. It's over, the duty's done. Go on home. But they're still there, talking to each other. Why don't they leave? Because the longer they stay and complicate the scene, the longer I might watch, and neither of us needs the grief. We all have to go home, before ...

Before one of the men walks over to my dad, who now looks more spooked than all of us put together. Oh no. Trust me, mister, this won't end well. Gently back away, and whatever you do, don't tap the glass. I'm telling you, don't do it.

Okay, in reality, I'm just inwardly chanting it to myself, but am desperately hoping the universe will scream it on my behalf. Listen dude, if you know what's good for you.

But what's this guy do? Extends his hand ... which my dad stares at for a few seconds, not sure if it's meant for him. But it is. A handshake for the gravedigger?

My dad takes off his dirty glove and shakes hands with the man, who appears to be thanking him. For digging a hole? Then, track two of my cerebral soundtrack kicks in: "*He gives people their final resting place.*"

Yes, he does. And from the looks of it, a unique sense of comfort in seeing the care that goes into it. That's reason enough for a handshake.

And reason enough for my dad to take a second to compose himself after the guy leaves.

And reason enough for me to keep watching.

6

LAST IN TRANSLATION

"It's all gibberish."

That's how she put it. And no words could ring more true at this very moment. Not that she knew they would pertain to this situation. But Grandma must have known these words would apply somewhere, sometime, and therefore, tucked them into my back pocket for just such occasions.

See, my grandma lived with us for about a year, before she was moved into an assisted-living home. It was an experiment that was destined to fail, but one that deserved some kind of shot, for karma's sake. So Grandma camped out in her own room downstairs, reading Western paperbacks by some guy named L'Amour (who sounds suspiciously French, and what the hell do the French know about cowboys?), and watching baseball on the Spanish-language station. That's what sparked the comment above, when I asked her why she kept the sound turned down for nine innings.

"It's all gibberish," she spouted.

I've since learned to employ that viewpoint on pretty much everything. While Grandma may have occasionally wandered off the reservation in her later years, she did have this one theory nailed. If the world around you makes no sense, don't blame yourself. Blame the language barrier. Stop and consider how much easier life would be if we could just bypass all the scoldings, unsolicited advice and boring invites we ever received by conveying two simple words: "No comprendé."

Coupled with the fact that Grandma wore hearing aids, she also had the ever-convenient option of simply "turning down and tuning out" the world whenever it became too loud and distracting. This technique must be one of the unspoken rules, and few perks, of getting old. Whenever Grandma's friends (or "old biddies" as she called them) would get together for their weekly card game, it was like watching a fascinating, slow motion car crash. Forget the cards, my bets were always about who had their hearing aid turned off versus who was simply faking it with "selective" hearing.

Think about how amazing that skill would be to constantly toy with people—like being a spy, with those high-tech earpieces, where you have to keep a straight face while somebody on the other end is giving you the order to blow away the poor slob sitting across from you. Sure, I know that's way more intense than a low-stakes game of "Go Fish," but the principle is still the same. Silence is power, and nobody exploits that theory better than old people. They acknowledge only what they want to hear, and they predictably get a free pass because they're old.

Much as I want to, I can't play that card, yet. When you're fifteen and ignore conversation, people instantly chalk it up to "attitude." I'm not saying they're wrong. I'm just saying that it's unfair to exclude all other possibilities, since there could be heaps of reasons why I'm blowing you off. As a society, are we so in need of immediate feedback that we can't wait it out once in a while?

"Answer me!" Mom demands.

Apparently, we are.

Mom has clearly bought into the whole "immediate feedback" thing. In that case, I will embrace the exact opposite approach.

"Huh?"

"What is your answer, Greer?"

Oh joy, now she's calling me by name. This discussion is not going away anytime soon.

Personally, I don't get it. I thought multiple choice tests were supposed to have at least three options: one downright useless answer, which you can immediately toss out, and two that are similar enough that you can't determine which is the right answer. That's usually the drill. So what happened here? Where's the useless option? Trust me, that would absolutely be my choice right now.

Instead, I'm expected to choose between two scenarios that are so ridiculously similar in their level of "non-fun," that to select either one will undoubtedly make me pine for the other, thinking I got massively screwed. Welcome to my life, people.

But before I launch into a hefty rambling about what miserable level of existence I will certainly suffer, let me just plead the Fifth … or some variation of it, since I tend to doze in History, and don't know all the finer points of the Fifth Amendment. I just know it's something designed to keep us from effing ourselves.

"I refuse to answer on the grounds it may obligate me," I announce.

Blank stares, until Mom speaks up. "Nice try. But no."

Despite her position, I'm heartened by the fact that she commended my effort, which means I could be onto something here. So I concoct a second attempt at escape.

"I refuse to make a choice that could unfairly show preferential treatment to either of you. Therefore, I abstain."

Dad seems mildly impressed by my line of reasoning. Mom's not buying it, though.

"We're letting you make a choice," she says. "So I suggest you do that, or we'll decide for you."

Let's face it, no teenager wants their parents in charge of their decisions, unless it involves pulling the plug or determining what credit card they're going to let you use whenever you've successfully blackmailed them into a "Buy me this or I'll spill my guts" purchase.

But when it comes to how to spend your spring break, there is no possible way you want to give up the reins on that one. So you try one irrational approach after another, until you listlessly throw in the towel … especially after it occurs to you that they own your towel, your bed, and virtually every inch of personal space you occupy within their house. You either give up or start paying rent.

In short, here are my options …

DOOR #1: Stuffing, delivering, and setting up flower

arrangements for the Bridezilla wedding (selfishly scheduled during my one week of spring freedom), which will invariably subject me to Mom's slave-driving tendencies, which pop up like zits whenever she's stressed out by an exceptionally bitchy client.

DOOR #2: Accompanying Dad on the road trip he now has to do to deliver some dead guy's ashes to a cemetery out of state. Mom is worried that Dad's temporary insanity hasn't fully run its course, which may cause him to drive off the road in a moment of surreal delusion. A backup driver for just such occasions would be helpful. Under normal circumstances, I would be giddy at the thought of getting behind the wheel. But the prospect of sharing the ride with an authority figure and a human ashtray is more than a little disconcerting.

"What's Door Number Three?" I implore.

Dad looks confused. He's obviously not been playing along at home. At least Mom has a vague idea of what I'm talking about.

"There isn't one. Those are your choices," Mom affirms.

The audience waits in breathless anticipation. I can practically hear a countdown clock in my head. *Tick, tick, tick.* Or maybe it's an internal timer because this situation is so volatile my head is about to explode. Hey, is that an option? Have I subconsciously invented a Door #3 to make a quick escape? Am I some sort of "argument savant" who's actually going to worm out of this through sheer will? It could happen, right?

TICK, TICK, TICK.

The internal noise becomes deafening. My theory that

I'm a secret genius is quickly fading. Which leads to my next terrifying thought …

What if I pick one and I hate it? But then what if I pick the other, and I hate that one even more? What if I end up hating myself because the one I picked is so much lamer than the other one might have been, but I'll never know for sure, because I no longer have the option to bail and go with the other one? Plus, my head would have exploded by then, which can't possibly be a good look.

My life has now been reduced to a theater of the absurd. Don't believe me? Fine, smartass. You choose, and see how thrilled you are. Either you get to live inside the manic chaos of a Japanese monster movie, with Bridezilla destroying everything in her wake, while your Mom spews some indiscernible, rapid-fire language that you can't begin to comprehend. Or you get to be the passenger clinging for dear life in a coyote cartoon where he drives the Acme van off a cliff, and instead of dynamite, there's a coffee can full of ash waiting to blow up when you hit the bottom. All the while, your friends who *got* a spring break are all off enjoying life and may be tempted to fill your vacancy in their social circle with someone new and momentarily fascinating because you went AWOL and that's how we are.

Yeah … either way, this blows.

"I'll take the road trip," I surrender, figuring a person reduced to powder is arguably less scary than a living, breathing mother on her last nerve. I look at it like this: ashes don't talk, Bridezillas scream. And since Dad is still in something of a catatonic state, he's not likely to be too chatty, so that's a huge bonus.

Between you and me, I don't understand why they can't just box up the guy's residue and put a few stamps on it. Unless there are some uptight laws about sending human remains through the mail? Some cheap jagoff with poor packaging skills probably blew that option for everyone. Anything to inconvenience me. Seriously, there's gotta be a solution to work around this.

I finally can't take the suspense and flag the obvious.

"Why are you driving him?"

"Because it's overtime, and we can use the money," Dad says matter-of-factly.

"No, I mean ... why can't you just stick him on an airplane? He's technically cargo."

"Because he was afraid of flying," Dad replies, miraculously holding a straight face.

Now, I'll agree I'm no rocket scientist, so there could be technical reasons why I shouldn't keep asking the obvious. But since I'm not paid to explore the mysteries of the universe, I'm damn well gonna take the shortcut.

"Considering that he's dead, do you really think he'll notice?"

There it is. The beat of silent hesitation, with the vacant eyes. Dad is pathetically trying to pull an old-geezer move and pretend he didn't hear me. But even Mom's ears are piqued, waiting for this one. She secretly loves it that her obnoxious teenage daughter raised the question that the obnoxious teenager lingering in her forty-something body was totally dying to ask. Dad realizes he's been tag-teamed and has no choice but to answer.

"His will stipulates he has to be driven," Dad clarifies.

Mom and I stare at him, incredulous.

"And he paid in advance," Dad throws in.

No doubt, the dearly departed naturally anticipated rounds of eye-rolling and sarcastic laughter at his final wishes. So by plunking down the money and making it legally binding, he left the funeral home with no choice. Since Dad's gardening skills have delighted the higher-ups, he was handpicked for the happy task. With the promise of overtime to ease the sting of this ridiculous exercise, he willingly "turned down and tuned out" all pesky little voices of reason.

Yes, it's now official … my dad is an old fart.

*

"I changed my mind."

I've heard it's a woman's prerogative, so I'm cashing in that chip. Liv never got that memo, or is employing selective memory to act like she's never caught wind of such a concept. Is it just me, or have you ever noticed how families do that? The whole "selective memory" thing? Over the years, stuff just gets magically filed away, then is either promptly buried, never to surface again (much like Dad's latest clients), or is systematically dug up and hauled out at just the right moment, to drive a point home (much like the expired guy in our upcoming road trip). In this case, Liv is alternately employing both techniques: having buried the notion that I'm allowed to change my mind, while simultaneously drilling it into my skull that, at one point, I *may* have said I would help her break the news about her pregnancy to our parents.

I don't recall the exact wording, but whatever I did say, it was in a moment of weakness and meant in more of an arbitrary way—not a "let's put something on the books" way. So now that she's trying to call out my generosity, I'm feeling a tad unmotivated.

"I'm just not sure it's the best time," I determine. "They're dealin' with a lot of stuff right now."

"Oh, and I'm not?" Liv shoots back.

I swear, talking to Liv is like playing a psychological game of "Twister." You never know how the conversation is going to bend, but it somehow contorts back around to her.

"I could really use some parental support right now," she says.

The gleam in her eye hints at a monetary angle, so I quickly point out, "You know they're broke, right?"

Liv scoffs, pretending to be offended. "That's not the support I'm talking about. I just … would appreciate their advice. That's all."

Now I know she's lying. Liv never wants advice from anyone, which is precisely why I'm gonna tell her what to do. Until, a thought hits me. I guess it should have been a somewhat obvious thought, given the circumstances.

"Are you thinking of not keeping it?"

Liv doesn't respond.

"Or not … *having* it at all?"

Liv throws up her hands, fighting off a mini-meltdown.

"Jeez, I don't know!" she shrieks. "All right? I don't know! I don't know what I'm thinking. I don't know what I'm feeling. I just …"

Liv's face tenses up, her voice trailing off, "I don't know."

And I have no words, because I'm stuck in the same boat. I don't know what to think or feel, either.

Liv notices my open suitcase, which provides a merciful diversion.

"Why are you packing?"

"It's a tragically long story," I say.

"Are you running away?"

"No, but thanks for the encouragement."

I explain how Dad got assigned to deliver the guy's ashes, Mom has to suck up to a bride from hell, and I had no appealing alternatives. The mere thought of untold hours in the party mobile has coaxed me to pack the stuffed teddy bear I haven't used as a crutch since I was four years old. Yes, like a child, I'm bringing a stuffed animal for moral support ... and to have at least one other inanimate object to make conversation with, since Dad will have to sleep on occasion.

It's no surprise that Liv gets my choice. She would never have the patience to put up with a whiney bride. It'd be an all-out brawl in record time. As for the alternative—carpooling with the dearly departed—most rational people are too creeped out to admit that as their actual preference, so they just clam up. Except for my sister, who's never at a loss for words.

"I don't get this whole 'death' thing," Liv claims. "What's the point?"

I didn't say they were *logical* words.

"I think it's a requirement," I surmise. "For, like ... *everyone.*"

"I get that. I just don't see why it needs to be a big production, with hoopla and sendoff, and all that. When it's your time, it's your time. Just grow a pair and go."

Hmmm. There's a thought. On the one hand, it's more than a little compelling to imagine going out with a public bang, and who would show up at your funeral, and who would genuinely cry compared to who would fake it, and who would feel most guilty for being such an absolute ass to you in life. You know what I'm talkin' about. You know you've wondered.

But maybe there's something to be said for quietly going out the side door. *"Elvis has left the building."* Five words that still pack a punch, because they ache of missed opportunity. At the same time, they scream decisiveness. Elvis had his own schedule. It's not his fault you didn't read the fine print. So you're left behind with lingering thoughts of "What do I do now? How do I make it right? Dang, was I so overbearing that he chose to bolt instead?"

Face it—some people just aren't into long goodbyes. They get in, they get out. Done.

Still, I never would have pegged Liv as one of those people. She always wants to be the center of attention. Why should a little detail like mortality ruin everything? In fact, wouldn't death be her ultimate showpiece? The guilt factor alone would be enticement enough for her to plan the entire thing ahead of time, complete with guest list, playlist and party favors. Considering there are only a few events in life that bring together ALL of our friends and family—some of whom we'd most want to stick it to in a public setting—it would seem that funerals truly are the final hurrah. The last real chance to celebrate the miracle that is us.

The fact that Liv, of all people, is not buying into this idea is beyond shocking.

"So, you don't want anybody to make a big to-do when you die?" I pose.

"Of course not," Liv assures.

I dare say I'm somewhat impressed by her maturity … until the other shoe inevitably drops.

"That would spoil all the fun," she adds.

Yes, that's the operative word. *Fun.* Liv reveals that her game plan for the afterlife includes "haunting" those who've made her miserable in this life. Oh, and the best part—wait for it—is that not only does she intend to invade their homes, psyches, and daily lives, but she's adamant that this choice is one that's readily in her control. Forget harps and little wings; Liv's goal is to be a "cold spot" in the personal space of any insufferable dingleberry she's ever known. And to hear her tell it, that list is painfully long, so the whole "paranormal" thing could take a while.

"It's genius," Liv posits. "No funeral means they'll think they never have to own their nastiness. But little do they know, that's when the party will kick into overdrive."

Liv beams in anticipation, convinced that this plan is downright foolproof. If she weren't smiling so much— actually, it's more of a sickly grin—I might not be so inclined to be a downer at this point. But if I don't make an effort to act in her best interest, I could end up on Liv's doomed shitlist—and that is not a place I want to be. *Ever.*

"You do realize that some of those people may already be dead, by the time you go?" I point out.

"Meaning?" Liv feverishly stares at me.

"Um," I utter, trying not to crawl under the bed. "Meaning that if you're hanging out on Earth, they'll be someplace else. And then you might get kinda ... *bored?*"

Evidently, this contingency hadn't been taken into account. Liv hates to be bored. To spend eternity like that would be a fate worse than death. The only real assurance that she could effectively torment every single person she had in mind, would mean that she would have to die, like, *now*. And knowing that she has a mani/pedi scheduled for the afternoon—not to mention sweet concert tickets for next week—the immediacy of that circumstance is simply not practical.

Liv ponders her destiny, still clinging to her diabolical scheme. "When the time comes, I'll just have to move between both worlds. There's bound to be a monthly pass of some sort, and if not, I'll petition to make one. It could be a hot item."

Truer gibberish has never been spoken.

7

LAST MAN STANDING
Or
"How I Spent My Spring Break," by Erger Sarazen

DAY ONE: Monday.

"He's in a tiny coffin?"

"No," Dad replies. "That's just a box. His urn is inside."

I cast a skeptical look at the box: your average, square, nondescript packing box.

"You sure he wasn't like a mini vampire?"

"Don't be insulting," Dad says.

He loads our luggage into the van: your average, square, nondescript company van. I was hoping for one of those tricked-out conversion vans. You know, the ones with the leather seats, flat screens and lounge vibe. No such luck here, as I sourly concede that we're not rappers.

"Where's he gonna sit?" I ask.

Dad slants an eyebrow. "What do you mean?"

"Well, the guy paid for all this. He should at least have scenery, don'tcha think?"

"This isn't a vacation," Dad dismisses.

"Not for you," I agree. "Certainly not for me. But he's pretty much on permanent vacation now. The hard part's over, he's just hangin' out."

"Greer … this man deserves our consideration."

"So you're leaving him in a stuffy box?"

Dad sighs and opens the flaps of the box. "There. Happy now?"

I stare at the contents. "It looks like a vase, with a lid."

"It's an urn," Dad says.

Urn? Who came up with that word? It's like, three letters. It's a mini-word. Seeing as this thing is designed to hold the remnants of an entire person, you'd expect it to have a more imposing name. Take "sarcophagus," for example. Even though I tend to doze in History, I fuzzily remember talk of them in ancient Egypt, and things never seemed to end well when they were around. So to chew on that word means ever-enchanting thoughts of mummies and ancient curses.

Plenty of other words are just as formidable.

"Crypt": A beady-eyed skinny guy, inviting you to a land where no one enjoys the bedtime stories.

"Mausoleum": Cold, white, stoned. Insert "Random Trust Fund Baby" here.

"Tomb": Simply nothin' good to be had with that word.

So to try to lump a mini-word like "urn" into that mix, just doesn't work. Personally, I don't see how "vase" is all that far off the mark, in light of the task at hand.

"So you're gonna plant this thing?"

"He's not a fern," Dad snaps. "He's a person."

I beg to differ. "At this point, he's more like powder."

"That's enough, Greer," Dad demands. "Don't be disrespectful."

Disrespectful? Since when is speaking the truth disrespectful? I remember being told that lying showed a lack of respect, whereas the truth is all shiny and pretty and rewarded. Has that much changed since I was twelve? I hold up that year as the benchmark, simply because that's the age when I got grounded for a month for lying about who brought the shaving cream.

Let me back up. So, one day, a bunch of us girls decided to have a shaving cream fight after school. There was no real reason why, except that we were twelve, and found things like shaving cream fights to be culturally stimulating. But being girls, we planned it ahead of time—picking the day, choosing just the right outfit (nothing too nice that would get ruined, but still something cute and breathable), and initiating a guest list which, of course, included only the cutest boys in school. It was a perfect plan, and almost perfectly executed, except for one slight flaw ...

Namely, "Side Pocket," a.k.a. Mr. Cribber, Assistant Principal at my junior high. Simply put, if Ginormous is Bigfoot, then Side Pocket would be the Chihuahua she carries in her purse: skinny, wide-eyed and habitually nervous. His original name was "Cueball," since his head was bald as a baby's bottom. So such a label was an obvious choice. That was the problem. It became too risky to use the name in public conversation, since all it would take is one chatterbox and the jig would be up in no time. Consequently, "Side Pocket" was born.

It was kind of brilliant, really. Teachers just assumed it was a catch phrase of some sort. They didn't put it together that it was code for a pointy-eared attack dog. I *so* wish I could take credit for the name, but that honor belongs to Gavin Brunman, who earned an early release from "name jail" by coming up with something so inspired it magically put to rest his own unfortunate nickname: "Bun Man." Gavin's family had a pool table in the basement, so he wisely built upon the "Cueball" theme to dream up just the right tag.

Everyone was so blown away, it immediately elevated Gavin's social status, and the "Bun Man" label was no more. Until he was a freshman in high school, that is, and then it resurfaced again during "hell week." Nothing could save him after that. We all just had to mournfully look away, as Bun Man pined for his days of fleeting popularity. God, we're a fickle bunch.

Anyway, back to me …

Side Pocket wasn't amused by our little stunt and came charging out of the school as fast as his boney legs could carry him. Since we were all much younger than the artist formerly known as Cueball, our legs ran a lot faster. We all scattered like cockroaches, but there were enough traitors amongst the group that fingers were pointing in no time. I was brought in for a lineup in Side Pocket's office.

"Where were you Tuesday at 3:42 p.m.?" he spat.

"I don't have a watch," I said. Note, I was still telling the truth at that point.

"What's that got to do with anything?" Side Pocket groused.

"Well, you're being very specific on the time. And since the school board never coughed up money for a sundial, I can't really speculate."

To this day, I firmly maintain that I had a legitimate argument on that one. But as usual, Side Pocket's undies were in a bunch. He glared like a frazzled screech owl.

"You can't blame this on something that wasn't there. But according to witnesses, *you* were."

He waited for me to confess, as if that was gonna happen. "Were you there, Greer?"

In dissecting the phrasing of the question, I felt justified to skirt around it, since—at that particular point in time—I was going through one of my many tween phases and inwardly calling myself "Alexandra." So in that respect, the accusation didn't apply to me.

"No," I confidently answered.

"*NO??* After all this, you expect me to believe you weren't there?"

I just needed to let him simmer long enough to spill over.

"I'm sorry, who are we talking about again?" I feigned interest.

"You, Greer! We're talking about you!"

He conveniently took the bait. By stating that the conversation pertained to *Greer*, instead of my newly adopted persona, I figured there was ample wiggle room to deny everything.

My parents, however, didn't agree, and sided with the pocket. Thus, began my month of virtual house arrest, and the nonstop reminders that lying will not be tolerated. To this day, I adamantly stand by my case that "Alexandra" should not have been punished for any sketchy undertakings by that "Greer" chick. But I determined it was easier to meet them halfway, rather than ruin any potential for them ever letting me borrow the car. I've chewed on this bitter pill for three and a half years, but now ...

Here I am, speaking the truth, and still I get scolded. Is there no winning in this dictatorship? Not to mention, Dad chastised me by name just now, which parents do to underscore their point. Little does he know, I'm in no mood for a verbal mugging. Game on.

"For this trip, I'd like to be known as 'Erger.' Please make a note of it."

Factoring in that Dad is now at the wheel of a company vehicle, and we're at cruising speed on the freeway, perhaps it's not the best time to open that wound.

"We're back to this? Are you serious?" Dad asks.

"*Dead* serious. A tad fitting, given the circumstances."

"All right, knock it off," Dad grumbles. "Your name is your name. Your mother and I chose it for you."

"That's my point," I argue. "*You* chose it. I didn't."

Dad sighs, clearly not wanting to have this discussion again. So he reaches for every parent's easy out ...

"When you're eighteen, you can change it then."

There it is, the magic number. Whenever parents have no idea how to do battle with a teenager, they play the "when you're eighteen" card. "When you're eighteen, you can get a tattoo." "When you're eighteen, you can pierce whatever you want." "When you're eighteen, you can move out and pay your own bills." I don't know about ancient societies (since I tend to doze in History), but I'd venture to guess that the "eighteen" bone has been tossed around for centuries.

"What's the big whoop? Why can't I call myself something else?" I plead.

"Because a name matters," Dad insists. "It's not something you should just pick out of thin air."

Tell that to celebrities having babies.

"In my own defense," I say, "I've, at least, been trying to use the letters in my name."

Dad smiles, amused. "Yes, but it's not really working."

"Welcome to my world," I slump.

I look again at the urn, sitting in a box in the back seat. Even that thing has name options, since it could totally pass for a "vase." Life is so unfair.

I'm so bored I could scream.

We're in the middle of nowhere, I have no cell reception, and the radio is pure static. If deserted highways weren't full of snakes and serial killers, I'd fling myself out the door. We had scenery for a little while, but that's over.

Since I'm not used to having people in my head, I forgot to mention that we live in Colorado. Boulder, to be exact. Go ahead, be jealous. Even Mork was like, "I'm totally crashing here."

Apart from already being colossally fabulous, one of the best things about Boulder is that you get snow days. Any kid will tell you—snow days are like nectar from the gods. Along with getting you out of school, they give you one more reason to make snowmen (like you needed that, duh). And if we're all going to be forced to navigate the slippery slope of modern society, we might as well snowboard while doing it.

There's also hiking and rock climbing, for those days when I get off the couch. Not that I know the specifics of rock climbing, but I count it as a skill ever since I had to climb on top of a neighbor's garage to dodge a drunken bear who'd wandered into the neighborhood, after imbibing on a not-quite-empty bottle of malt liquor in someone's recycling bin. It was only once I was on top of the structure that I remembered bears can climb, too. Thankfully, this one was tipsy enough to overlook that detail.

Another neighbor, Emma Petrovi, squealed that she saw the whole episode, and claimed it was just a big, lumbering dog. But she was watching from a distance and wears some schizzo colored contacts, so I beg to differ with her account. It was a friggin' bear. And believe me, if you see a bear anywhere in your general vicinity, you'll tap into survival mode you never knew you had, while wishing you wore adult diapers. I'm still alive, so something worked. Probably the malt liquor.

Moving along, now we're past the scenery, since we're driving this guy to someplace in Michigan. Which means a fascinating trek through the Midwest. Yes, this is how I will spend my spring break—on wide-open roads with a loopy parent in a clunker van, and a dusty passenger inside something that looks like a popcorn tin from Dracula's attic.

Growing desperate, I start scouring the van for anything to keep me occupied, which is a challenge of monumental proportions since I'm lazy enough to keep the effort within arm's reach. In the van's console, I find a stack of business cards that Digby provided Dad, just in case any networking opportunities arise. I can't tell if Dad is proud to have new business cards, and is discreetly attempting to show them off, or if he tossed them into the console as an afterthought.

"What is a Cemetery Technician?" I wonder aloud.

"Huh?"

"Your business cards. They say Cemetery Technician. What is that?"

Dad dodges the question. "Oh, uh … it can mean various things."

"Is your work technical? Being a technician and all?"

"Um …," Dad waffles. "A little bit, I guess."

Dad takes the cards and pops them into the glove box, trying to avoid the subject. Something about the title tends to embarrass him—either because it's a load of bull, or that particular title is one that he never envisioned next to his name. It must be hard, training to be one thing, and then waking up one day and doing a completely different job that you never saw coming. In that case, acknowledging the title on a business card isn't exactly a thrill, as the acknowledgement makes it real.

Dad stays silent and just stares straight ahead. I'm never quite sure how to read him when he gets like this. Keeping quiet is the best thing I can do for him right now. But I can't help feeling like I should say something, as long as it doesn't sound too lame.

"Your boss must think you're doing a good job. To give you business cards, and all."

Dad reluctantly considers this reality, before brushing

it off. "They're easy enough to print now. Not the financial commitment they used to be."

That's Dad—constantly crunching the numbers. Back in the day, you had to order a whole box of five hundred or more, which sometimes outlasted the job itself. I open the glove box and take out a card, examining Digby's handiwork.

"It's good card stock," I observe. "That's key, since presentation is everything. Liv gave me one of the cards Herman made at the Hacienda. They were so flimsy they could be dinky cocktail napkins."

Dad doesn't answer, but the corner of his lip curls up just enough to speak for him. He either sees the humor, or the fact that he is genuinely appreciated. Either way, it's a momentary bonus.

Meanwhile, Dad tries tuning the radio, while I resume searching the van for anything the least bit fascinating. As you might expect, it's not going well. I silently beg the universe to pity me, when my eyes land on the only remotely stimulating thing in the vicinity. The urn. Yes, you heard right. Call it my sad reality. Call it morbid fascination. Call it ...

"William."

Dad still fiddles with radio. "What?"

"His name is William."

Dad leaves the radio stuck on static. "Who?"

I grab some paperwork that pokes out of the box and start reading.

"The guy in the urn. William Parkner."

"Put that away!" Dad snatches the paperwork.

"What's the problem?"

"You shouldn't be snooping!" he nags.

"I wasn't! It was just sitting there."

Wow, Dad's pissed. His neck is contracting and bulging like a blowfish, where the vein looks like it could explode any second. I seriously hope this isn't one of those insurance exclusions, because it doesn't look promising. And since I kinda zoned out in that CPR class, there's a real chance I could screw him up even worse.

Given the patently delicate nature of this predicament, a mature adult would likely address this moment with sensitivity and calm reflection. But I'm a teenager, so you get what you get.

"Are you freaked out 'cuz you guys have the same name?"

Dad immediately clams up, pretending that I won't notice him ignoring the subject. Not a chance. Especially after I shut off the static that's still coming out of the radio. Now Dad's really coming unhinged. With no artificial noise to fill the air, he pulls such an "old man" move I can barely restrain myself.

He starts whistling.

Are you kidding me? Think about it—who do you know who "whistles" on a regular basis? Gardeners? Delivery men? The whole myth that people whistle because they're happy is a total crock. They whistle to kill time ... or other things, like my patience.

In this case, Dad is whistling to kill the conversation. Since he and Mom are always telling me to be more committed to things, I waste no time in resuscitating it. Maybe that CPR class wasn't a total wash.

"You're weirded out by that, aren't you?"

"I am not!" he lies.

"Yes you are. A guy with your name is the consistency of cement mix and living in a trophy. That bugs you."

"Stop talking about him like that!" Dad demands. "He was a person. Treat him with dignity!"

"Calling him by name is dignified," I contend.

"You can call him Mr. Parker."

"Why would I do that?"

"Because it's polite," Dad says.

"Actually, it's pretty rude, since his name is Park*ner*."

Dad grabs the paperwork, scanning it again. Now, keep in mind, he's still driving. So purely in the interest of safety, I selflessly offer to do the responsible thing.

"Want me to drive while you read?"

"No!" Dad stews.

Man, he's fired up. I briefly flirt with elaborating on the Steaming Buddha's mantra of "Don't Drive Angry," but worry that may further strain Dad's hairpin boundary between sanity and batshit crazy.

He jams the paperwork back into the box.

"You really hate that paperwork, don't you?" I notice.

Dad shoots me a look, as I realize it's not the physical paper, itself, but rather, *what it says* that is loathed. Uh huh, I took in more data than I let on. The name thing was just all I could get out before Dad went spastic. I happened to catch a glimpse of William's birth date, and it turns out, he was only a few years older than Dad. My dad's in his mid-forties ... although I lost track of the actual number. But I know that's the general ballpark. So William wasn't all that old, and now look at him. I mean, yeah, he was a little old, but he wasn't *old* old. He wasn't the kind of old where your false teeth plop out after you've fallen asleep with your mouth open, and a moth is buzzing around your head, and no one is quite sure if the moth was in the room to begin with, or if it literally came out of you. My grandma was that old, and trust me, once you've seen the moth conundrum, you can never *un*see it.

"Can he sit up here with us?" I ask.

"What??"

"You said to treat him with dignity. Right now, he's stuck in a box."

"He's not stuck! He's—"

Dad stops himself from stating the obvious.

Even though I know what he was gonna say, I lean forward, looking at him with wide-eyed innocence. The whole thing is classic. A minute ago, I was begging for anything to keep me entertained. Who knew I'd stumble upon the Holy Grail of pissing contests?

"He's what?" I play it to the hilt.

Dad can't spit it out. So I do.

"Dead?"

Dad doesn't respond, his jaw apparently unable to open anymore.

"So?" I taunt.

Let me just add a personal sidebar, that my favorite mini-word has to be "So." It's only two letters, but the versatility is mind numbing. Depending on your tone, it's the most intimidating use of alphabetical real estate out there. Just stop and consider the dizzying array of options: snotty, inquisitive, demanding, nosey. The sheer beauty of it is that each option is equally effective, with its own caustic sting. It may be mini, but it's massive.

Dad sits there looking at me, his mind racing with a million potential responses. Again proving its intoxicating effect, he reaches for the magic term.

"So??" he mocks, invoking the parental inflection of *"Hey, you started this, and I have nowhere to take it. Your turn."* Man, I love that mini-word.

"*SO* ... the scenery's better up here," I point out. "We could open the lid, and—"

Whoa! Before Dad can stop me, I proceed to open the urn's lid, and am horribly unprepared for what's inside. To think of an impressionable teenage mind being imprinted by such a ghastly image is more than a little disconcerting.

"*He's in a plastic bag??*" I cringe.

No judgment, but I've never been in therapy, and I'd like to keep it that way. So for once, I'm hoping Dad will choose to start talking, because I'm severely wigging.

"Yes, to contain the remains," Dad says. "What did you expect?"

Oh, gee, I don't know. I just figured the guy was kicking back in his urn—maybe with a small couch, some lamps, a little smooth jazz. Like a tiny home.

But no. He's more like ... gravel. In a baggie. It's such a trip that a human being can be reduced to this. I've heard the whole "ashes to ashes" thing, but I never fully processed what it meant. NOTE TO SELF: when they say "ashes," they're *SERIOUS.*

Dad notices my twitchy look, wondering, "Are you okay?"

"Um ... I guess so."

To his credit, Dad emerges from his cerebral siesta

long enough to catch on that this moment is a bit substantial for me, so he does something completely unexpected.

"Maybe I will take you up on your offer to drive," he says. "Would you mind?"

He has to ask? I stare at him, realizing ... no, he doesn't. He's being polite. Remember what I said about Dad being a gentleman? And having that closeted "cool" side? This just proves I was right, since he's pulling over to switch seats. Who knew all it would take to get the car keys was opening a lid.

Urn. Vase. Popcorn tin. Whatever ... I just found my new lucky charm.

8

LAST FRONTIER

DAY TWO (Part One): Tuesday.

A hose. A tumbleweed. A clown.

Welcome to the boonies.

Because I'm a giver, I'll spare you the wearisome particulars and provide just the highlights. I use that term loosely, since the "highlights" of this little experiment are basically the scraps of what would be "lowlights" in any realm where free will is an option.

It started with a "clink." Then a "whoosh." Then a curse word. Not from me, but from Dad. Of course I was tempted to join in, but the stream of expletives in my head has been playing like gangsta rap ever since we left, so profanity is more like white noise at this point. Pretty soon, I'm gonna have to learn another language just to make it interesting again.

But hearing Dad spout a little potty mouth this morning did ring in my ears, simply because it's so disarmingly convenient. Especially when he threw out a few choice words, once it became obvious just how screwed we were. You never know when such a card may need to be whipped out of the ol' back pocket, when you're being reprimanded for some indiscriminate act of bad behavior. So it's always handy to have one more tool in the arsenal.

As for how the day has played out so far, I don't even know why I'm surprised. It had to be a lemon. Why would they bother to give us a van that worked? That would make too much sense. Fate had predetermined that any equation would add up as such: Crappy Van + Live Employee + Dead Client + Reluctant Guest = Stranded.

I sat on the bumper, watching a tumbleweed blow across the highway, while Dad talked to the "Roadside Assistance" guy. Grandma used to call it the "Auto Club," which sounds so much classier than what I was looking at. The club we got didn't appear to be too picky about membership, since this guy looked like a mash-up of Side Pocket, Ginormous, and the Steaming Buddha all rolled into one: bald head, hairy arms, and sweat stains. Not to mention a spare tire that had nothing to do with the van.

That weed was furiously tumbling. Where the hell was it going? And why couldn't I go too?

"He's gonna tow us into town," Dad said.

"He can't fix it?" I groaned. "What's the problem?"

"A hose."

"Yeah, I know we're hosed. I knew that before we left."

"No, that's the problem," Dad explained. "It needs a new hose."

If only it were that easy. Sure enough, once we got into town, that's when everything really went south. As I clung to the faint hope that we might be able to be underway by the afternoon, the unthinkable happened. Or, for this trip, it was more like the *inevitable* happened.

In short, Bozo dodged the weed and slammed into the fender.

"That clown hit me!" Dad growled.

"Sir, there's no need for insults," the cop said.

"*Insults?* He's a clown! Look at him!"

Sitting on the curb, smoking a cigarette and looking even scarier than they routinely do, was a clown. An ACTUAL clown, who swerved to avoid a tumbleweed (I swear it was the same one that was tormenting me along the prairie). In a fit of overcorrecting, the clown proceeded to ram into the back fender of the van as the tow truck sat at a red light—one mere block from the service station, which is where we are now.

Dad's talking to a cop, the van is toast, and I'm staring at a clown lighting up rolling papers with the flames of hell. It reminds me of a wacko Italian film I once caught while flipping through the channels one night. I didn't understand those scenes, either.

Did I mention the best part? The clown's only half-dressed. No, not like half-naked. Trust me, I'd be in another type of van heading to the nearest nuthouse if that were the case. No, he's just half-clown. His face is painted, but he's in sweatpants, flip-flops with socks, and a concert T-shirt from some '80s' hair band. The rest of his clown uniform is in his trailer at work, because somebody in charge thinks that a baggy bed sheet with polka dots and fuzzy buttons is much too valuable to leave the premises.

Sadly, his pilgrimage back to the required wardrobe was diverted when the weed came along and made the clown paranoid. I'll let you draw your own conclusions here, since it can't be much of a stretch. Suffice it to say, the clown has proven this morning that, yes, shit does happen and it does, indeed, roll down hill ... right into the back of our van.

We're not going anywhere, anytime soon. The clown hosed us. Even more than the hose itself.

"Sorry, man," the clown mumbles.

Yeah, right. That apology is almost as weak as his fashion sense. Maybe it's the cigarette dangling from his lip liner, or the smoke filtering out of his red, bulbous nose, or the fright wig of curly hair that looks like spaghetti on high alert. Nothing about this Boozo screams sincerity. Especially when he tries to extend what can only be described as an olive branch that's already died on the vine.

"Here are some comp tickets to the rodeo tonight."

I'm not making this up. I wish I were.

No, the circus isn't in town. That would be redundant, since the locals don't bat an eye at the smoking clown on the corner. In fact, his very presence doesn't seem to strike anyone as bizarre; or at least not bizarre enough to get any real attention. I'm sorry, but even in Boulder—with its fair share of oddballs—a smoking, headbanger clown on a street corner would generate a glance or two. But in farm country, clowns are like crop circles: they're disturbing, they pop up out of nowhere, and they're standard decor. So people learn to look the other way.

And now I'm being summoned to a rodeo. The

perfect cherry atop the melted mess of the day. I just stare at the tickets, with no intention of taking them. That would obligate me, wouldn't it? If I take them and don't show, would some honkin' "clown mafia" come after me? I could just see it—horns blazing, twenty of them pile out of a miniature car and hunt me down with snarling balloon animals. I only saw a few minutes of that Italian movie, but if ever it were going to give me a nightmare, I'm living it right now.

"Thanks," Dad says, taking the tickets. "That's very nice of you."

No, not really. Frankly, it's messed up. Dad is supposed to be my protector. He's obligated to be looking out for things like my safety and my sanity. Instead, he's committing me to a slow, painful decline by spiraling into audience participation at a barrel race.

Wait—do they have corn dogs at those things? Which reminds me …

"I'm hungry."

"What?" Dad looks at me.

"Food would be nice," I elaborate.

"Can't it wait?"

Apparently, *we're* the ones who'll be waiting. Turns out, the van needs some fender work to make it drivable again. Between that and the hose, it's gonna be at least a day or two. Who knew a clown car could do so much damage? You naively think they're like harmless little tin cans on wheels, but they're not. In this case, it was a death machine, because it killed any chance of us getting out of this rinky-dink town anytime soon.

Not to mention, Dad's stressing out about getting his

deceased client to his previously scheduled rendezvous with the afterlife. Considering there's a funeral on the books, we need to get our passenger to the chapel on time. Which means that this unforeseen delay now mandates that we hightail it out as soon as the van is roadworthy, and bust ass to get to Michigan.

Hang on—that means Dad will have no choice but to share driving duties with the only other passenger who could potentially take the wheel. Keeping in mind that the "client" no longer has dexterity, that would leave only one other option … ME.

Oh. My. God. This is perfect; what my grandma would have called "a bit of a pickle." Which reminds me …

"Can we go eat now?"

"You folks should get your stuff outta the van first," the mechanic drones.

Dad winces, unprepared to cozy up to the "client" beyond the trappings of the company vehicle.

"Uhhh …" he mutters, stalling.

"Sorry," the mechanic persists, "But we can't have none of them liability issues, after that whole 'electric car fiasco' a while back."

Wait—that fiasco was *these* guys?? I saw it on one of those "dumb criminal" shows. Remember when I talked about how we need stupidity to balance things out? This was a case of imbeciles on overdrive. Dim-witted criminals wreak enough havoc on their own, but when combined with a starstruck public, it's truly an epic fail. As for the fiasco in question, the basic equation was a stolen car, overloaded circuits, and microwave popcorn.

"That was *you* guys??" Dad marvels.

The mechanic sheepishly upholds that it wasn't entirely their fault, although the swirl of publicity tended to skew appearances. Basically, a couple of thieves from the big city were irked that gas prices ate up far too much of their stolen cash, and why should they spend all their funds on silly things like getaway fuel? So they stumbled upon one of those electric cars and thought, "Hey, now we're talkin'," and took it on a cross-country spin.

The joyride was ah-mazing, until the battery ran low, and it dawned on one of the thugs (for amusement, we'll call him "Einstein") that it might be handy to "charge" the car. But at that time, cow country wasn't exactly crawling with charging stations, so Einstein sought out help from the local repair shop (also known as "the place where I'm standing"). It was the first time these mechanics had seen an electric car, which only added to this recipe for disaster, since they were beyond mesmerized.

Einstein got a bit puffed up, considering that along the magical tour, he'd mistaken their carriage for an "Easy Bake Oven" of sorts. I emphasize the word "bake," since by that time, he was just high enough to start showing off his perceived genius, and offer a nonsensical demonstration of the car's amenities.

They recruited anything and everything that could be plugged into the cigarette lighter, along with every tool, utensil or dental filling that could generate a magnetic field. I'm vague on the methodology, but between the mechanics, the crooks and the outlets, there were plenty of short-circuits to go around.

Hilarity ensued, until one of the mechanics decided

that hunger took priority over the floorshow, and hit the start button on the microwave. From there, the story gets a bit murky. But, by all accounts, the electricity in the air was palpable. Only then did one of the mechanics realize that this level of frivolity went well beyond the bounds of user error, and maybe these guys weren't the actual owners ... and they'd just created Frankenstein. Or a variation of him, since rumor has it Einstein's accomplice now glows in the dark.

A whole new set of rules was implemented after the fact (to discourage any more glowing reviews), which means we promptly have to clear out the van. This requires us to take any personal effects, including passengers and luggage.

I would maintain that our pal in the urn is theoretically neither, but rather than call his boss to plead a gray area, Dad caves. Wonder if Dad thought this far ahead when Digby offered him the job. The look on his face suggests, "No." He just wanted the overtime.

Careful what you wish for. Now, it's *personal*.

*

"How many?"

"Two," I reply. "And a half."

The hostess waits for clarification. "You mean you need a booster chair?"

I mull it over. I am babysitting in a way, so getting a booster chair wouldn't necessarily be mocking the situation. But probably best to just stick to the facts.

"Nah. He won't be eating."

The hostess flashes a thoroughly confused smile. Dad's outside on a call, briefing Digby on how an evil clown sentenced us to temporary purgatory. So it's been left to me to get us a table for lunch.

The wheels on my suitcase squeak as the hostess leads me to a booth, while I juggle all the stuff I can carry from the van: a suitcase, a box, and one dead guy. The hostess pretends not to give me side eye, secretly debating if I'm a runaway or a fugitive. Her finger is just itching to dial the authorities, convinced that reward money somehow has to be involved. True, I am underage and was brought here against my will by an older man in a van, from which we had to confiscate human remains that we're transporting across state lines, in order to protect mechanics who are known for aiding and abetting criminals, since we were rammed from behind by a pothead clown who tried to bribe us. I admit—on paper, this doesn't look good.

In reality, this is just another day in the late-night bizarro Italian movie that has become my life. Still, the hostess is looking at me like her golden ticket to the good life, until Dad comes in and bursts her meddling little bubble, sending her back to her hostess station to await her next opportunity to get rich quick.

As for Dad, he's just trying to hold it together, since Digby's contract covers "Acts of God," but not "Acts of Clown." In other words, we have to get William to his rendezvous with destiny on time, or the whole prepaid arrangement could be null and void. Beats me how the financials work, but it's tricky enough that Dad and Digby are both sweating, since it's not like the client will just pop up after being misdiagnosed as dead and we'd all have a laugh over one big, happy accident.

Not that it can't happen—there's a reason those things are called "wakes." Though, in this case, I'd say we're done, unless this little Italian film takes a dark turn. Nothing would shock me at this point. I once saw this trippy horror movie about some artist whose hand gets chopped off in a car accident, and the hand goes flying out the window and lands in a prairie, and then it goes on a killing spree because it's so pissed that the guy didn't go back to look for it. You can't deny the hand had a valid point, considering that the guy punted and left it in the sticks. If I were a loose hand in that predicament, I'd be hostile, too. Sure, in theory, it could have tried to "thumb a ride." But who's gonna give a lift to an overly anxious appendage? That's what jock straps are for.

Speaking of horror movies, we're in a diner. Normally I'm all for anything fried, but seeing as no one here seems to have gotten the memo about rampant obesity, I've suddenly developed a taste for salad. Oh, how I sometimes wish I could enjoy the reckless abandon of teenage guys who eat like they have a tapeworm; the heedless euphoria that jackholes like Pester employ on a daily basis, sucking up donuts and candy bars faster than Grandma's old Hoover.

Yet, I am a feminine mind. I am higher functioning. I am almost woman. Hear me roar.

"The lettuce wedge, please," I primly announce.

The waitress—a cheery woman named "Lola"—jots the order with a stubby pencil wedged between her stubby fingers.

"Extra blue cheese, darlin'?"

"Why not," I shrug. Maybe it was her sassy, Midwest drawl—or maybe I've just lost the will to live—but my pillar of strength only goes so high.

"You kept bugging me about food, and *that's* what you order?" Dad scowls.

"And for you?" Lola grins.

"Patty melt and fries," he shamelessly responds.

Now I'm the one shooting sour looks. Honestly, the hypocrisy is staggering.

"You bust on *my* choice, and *that's* what you order?" I call him out.

"What? You're not the only one who's hungry."

He's only doing this because Mom's not here. She'd thoroughly be reading him the riot act if she were. Mom's been trying for the past year to get Dad on a healthier diet regimen. Not that he's fat. But Mom got worried that his prolonged unemployment was making him lose his motivation (ya think??) and that if things got too out of control, she'd end up being married to either a sloth or a sumo wrestler. Like I said, I kinda zoned in that CPR class, so unless Lola knows the drill, he's pretty much on his own here.

Dad sips his coffee while I chew the straw in my lemonade. It's all so tragically quaint. I look around and sigh, since collapsing would take too much effort. When I imagine what all my friends must be doing this week—going to movies, hanging out at the mall, endlessly surfing the web—oh, how I pine for my former life. Sure, it didn't readily scream "ambition," but at least it was fun in its own vapid way.

But this? Trapped in the jail of the great frontier, with no sign of freedom for who knows how long? What did I do in a past life that doomed me to this existence? Who did I wrong that I now have to sacrifice my one and only spring break to make amends? Dude, *how did I get dragged into this??*

And then, I remember. Oh yes, the lovely ultimatum that was forced upon me by my parents. "Be ridiculously bored, or be ridiculously bored."

I glare across the table at one-half of the accused. Dad's looking at his phone, pretending to check email when I know he's just playing Solitaire and purposely ignoring me. He doesn't want to talk because he knows I have every right to rip him a new a-hole for getting me into this mess. Avoidance is his only hope of me not making a scene.

Too bad, mister. There are other ways to play this. Watch me.

PLOP! Dad looks up from his phone and stares at the urn, which now sits on the table, in plain sight. I can see his jaw clenching; the little beads of sweat beginning to form on his head; the nervous tic starting around the edge of his upper lip.

"What do you think you're doing?" he keeps it to a dull roar.

"You said to treat him with respect," I point out. "Including him in our daily activities would be a start, wouldn't it?"

This is brilliant. Highly dangerous, but brilliant. Dad's over a proverbial barrel and he knows it. If we weren't in public right now, he'd go absolutely bonkers on me.

Instead, he has to act composed while I test the boundaries of his dwindling patience.

"This is not the time or place to bring that out into the open," he insists.

"*That?*" I coyly provoke. "You mean, 'William'?"

Boom! Right in the jugular. Now Dad's facial tic is at warp speed. I know I'm gonna pay dearly for this, but it's much too intoxicating to stop.

"That is his name, you know. Catchy, don't you think?"

"Greer, I mean it," Dad seethes.

"Of course, you don't have to call him 'William,'" I forge ahead. "There are variations, unlike other names which don't offer alternatives."

"*Stop it. NOW.*"

Not a chance. This is the most fun I've had all week.

"After all, 'William' is so formal," I dig in my heels. "How 'bout something more casual, like 'Willie' or ... '*Will*'?"

Before he can leap across the booth to strangle me, Lola comes over with the coffeepot.

"Refill?" she asks, then notices the coffeepot's alter ego. "Oh my. That is one of the prettiest vases I've ever seen."

I smirk in giddy satisfaction, while Dad's just trying to keep it together.

"Actually," I whisper, "it's our traveling companion."

Lola catches on, her jaw dropping in amazement.

"You mean that's one of them ... *dead person* things?"

I smugly nod, while Dad's psyche begins to dismantle. This must be a huge moment for Lola, since she calls over another waitress to share the experience.

"Hey, Charlene! Get over here! You gotta see this!"

Awesome. Now we're drawing crowds. Dad's mortified.

Charlene—a taller, less-plump version of Lola—comes over and jumps upon seeing the urn.

"Oh my Lord! Who is that?"

Charlene gives the urn a quick once-over, admiring the handiwork.

"Must be somebody famous, 'cuz that's mighty fancy."

"Ooh, is it Elvis??" Lola gushes.

Charlene interjects, convinced that she knows better.

"Nah, my cousin saw him at Indian bingo last week."

"Maude?" Lola reacts, puzzled. "I thought she was banned from that place?"

"The restraining order didn't mention the parking lot."

I'm no expert, but I'd venture to say that's a bit of magical thinking on Maude's part, since there's bound to be legal parameters listed somewhere. For now, the only details Lola's concerned with are the contents of the urn.

"Is it a celebrity? You can tell me. I swear I can keep a secret." She pretends to zip her lip, trying to prove a point.

"Me too," Charlene assures. "Believe me, if the cops knew all I know about Maude, they wouldn't waste paper on a restraining order. They'd just slap the cuffs on her and call it a day."

"Or five to ten years!" Lola snickers.

The women share a hearty laugh, as Dad gives them a blank look.

"Seriously, who is it?" Lola coaxes.

"We don't know the family tree," Dad sputters.

"You don't know who you're travelin' with?" Charlene presses.

It's a legitimate question. You wander into a diner, flashing a perdy lil' vase around, people are bound to be curious.

"His name is William," I say, as Dad's jaw drops. "But we didn't know him personally."

"You mean you stole him?" Lola gets all googly-eyed. "Like grave robbers?"

A dead body on the lam could be the most excitement this place has seen since the electric car fiasco. Unless you throw in Maude, and then God knows what we're dealing with. Yet, we are not criminals. Just criminally insane for ever going along with this harebrained proposal.

"No. But he's a grave*digger*," I point at Dad, who silently fumes.

I say with full confidence that the only reason I'm able to keep up this verbal assault is because we're in public and Dad has no money for bail.

"Oh my," Lola shivers. "I never met anyone with that job."

"Sure you have," Charlene clarifies. "Remember that fella with the harelip and sort of hunched back, used to come in here? Always ordered the tater tots, extra crispy?"

"You have tater tots?" I gleefully wake up.

"That fella dug graves, too," Charlene boasts.

"Ooh, he gave me the heebie jeebies," Lola cringes. "Had that lazy eye that used to roll around like a marble. I swear I never knew where to look."

Dad slumps, defeated, and tries to tune out again—not so easy with two yappy waitresses who can't shut up about the resident hardware.

"You know, my Great Aunt Myrtle used to keep the ashes of her dead husband Earl in one of them things," Charlene recalls. "Right smack up on the mantle. She carried on about him like he was the salt of the earth."

Lola gets choked up, patting her heart.

"That's until she found love letters he'd written to an old girlfriend, talking about putting Crisco in belly buttons and other places where the sun don't shine," Charlene spills the whole, sordid story. "She decided he was no better than a snake at a picnic, just slithering around for all the tasty treats he could get. Next thing you know, the lid came off that urn and it became a vase."

"Good heavens," Lola braces. "What happened to Earl?"

"Nobody knows." Charlene eyes the room, leaning in as if sharing a state secret. "But a new cement sidewalk did get put in near the shed. *Co-in-cidence??*"

"Talk about stiffing someone," Lola snorts.

The women bust out laughing again. It seems Great Aunt Myrtle not only had a bit of a temper, but also an agenda. Specifically, walking all over a monument to her philandering husband. As for me, I have more modest goals in mind. Specifically, a monument to comfort food.

"Can I add some tater tots to my order?"

9

LAST RESORT

**DAY TWO (Part Two): Still Tuesday.
Yee Haw.**

"How many nights?"

"Eternity."

Oh wait, that's my subconscious talking.

"One," Dad says.

"I reckon you want two keys?" the motel clerk grumbles.

What's his problem? Did a hoarder convention wipe them out?

"Uh ... *yah*," I snottily retort.

Dad doesn't even scold me for that one. We just got here and he's already had a gut full of this guy ... who's evidently had a gut full of everything consumable within a fifty-mile radius. Seriously, pregnant women have less of a bulge. What's weird—or rather, "weirder," since there are so many weird things about him—is that he's not massive all over. But *damn*, that is one honkin' beer belly (or "Milwaukee Tumor," as Grandma would call it). I dare say he could even give the Buddha a run for his money, if either were inclined to run.

I stare at his plastic nametag—"Walter"—and wonder what could have decimated his life's dreams enough to lead him here. Did a Ginormous long ago torpedo his ambition, telling him that he was "uninspired" and "slacking?" Did he then pick up a remote control, never to do heavy lifting again? Or was he the valedictorian of his class, derailed by some bad mushrooms at a frat party? A one-time indiscretion that caused him to lose his scholarship and wind up angry and bitter, aching for the hopes that vanished on a whim?

"Coffee and donuts are out at 6:00 a.m.," Walter proudly announces. "Tomorrow is sprinkles day."

He beams like a kid on Christmas. Never mind. Walter's livin' his dream: "Slumlord."

Yeah, yeah … I know it's wrong to be judgmental, but give me a break. I'm in high school, and we all know high school is the original breeding ground for judgment. Add water daily and watch your shallow garden grow. And unlike the lump sum specimen before us, I still have a shot at moving on to greener pastures. Or at least a pasture, since I saw one on the edge of town.

Just be glad we didn't stop at the "campground" slash "trailer park," or I wouldn't have a shred of civility. Not that I have anything against communing with nature—and I'm all for convenience—but I firmly take the stance that toilets do not belong on wheels. Man has already done enough to screw up the natural order of things. Mobile crappers are just shaking our fist at the universe.

I'll spare you my commentary on the sights and smells during the walk down the hall to our motel room, since there are only so many avenues to effectively describe the striking color scheme of orange and brown. I was hoping for a minimum of "shabby chic," but obviously they went for "shabby, forget the chic." Words completely fail me, as did their decorator.

I look at my suitcase and debate whether to unpack. Part of my dejected self wants to be surrounded by the few creature comforts I brought, clinging to a ray of hope amidst this sad, alternate realm now holding us captive. But another part of me is terrified that if I do unpack, the room will suck up my stuff like a bloodthirsty sponge, and any ties to my former life will break faster than that paper toilet seat cover.

Which brings me to my next point. I may not travel a whole lot, but I've seen enough movies about weary tourists ending up at creepy roadside motels to know that in a small town, madness is baked into the fringe. The locals don't see it, because they're surrounded by it every day. But it's definitely there, just waiting to snap. Which is what creates that sense of paranoia for the sane, normal people who happen to be passing through, because they get it that the town is whacked … and if they don't leave soon, they will be, too.

Let's be honest—those movies never end well. If there's a big enough star in the lead role, they usually survive. But everyone else is toast. And even sometimes when there IS a big star, they get offed at the beginning just to make you super paranoid and shriek, "*WTF kind of movie is this?*" But by that time, you've already taken out a sizeable loan to cover the jumbo popcorn and soda you just bought, so leaving isn't an option, no matter how much you're freaking out.

Even when you're watching at home, then you're like, "Well, this blows because now I'm on the hook for the pay-per-view," so you feel forced to stick it out. Or you can't be bothered to drag yourself off the couch and go all the way back to the grocery store kiosk to return the disc you just rented because now you're way too terrified to leave the house, where a stranger is probably hiding and is going to call you any minute from a phone in another room. Your only choice is to throw something at the TV and just curl up into a ball and cry. And then wait for the sequel.

Anyhoo ... where was I? Oh, unpacking.

"Here are your shoes," I tell Dad, handing him a shoebox.

"What?" he asks, confounded. "That's not mine."

"It's not?"

"No. It's not yours?" he inquires.

A shoebox? Is he kidding? I'm not nearly that organized. I was ready to toss my stuff into a shopping bag until Mom forced me to use a real suitcase.

I shake my head, as a deafening silence falls over the room. It's official. The madness is setting in. Ut oh—where's my friggin' teddy bear? Behind the chair with a machete??

"Where'd that come from?" he warily eyes the shoebox.

"It was with ... *that*."

I point to the "bigger" box. Uh huh, that one. The box that's not for shoes, but for the rest of the person that the feet used to be attached to.

"I just grabbed stuff out of the van," I say.

Ladies and gentlemen, after a long absence, we are pleased to welcome back to our stage the incoherent stylings of ... "Zombie Dad!" Turn it up. He's *baaaccck,* along with vacant stare and mumblings that don't resemble anything close to English. So, once again, I have to do the talking.

"Maybe it popped out of the box when the clown rammed us," I theorize.

On the surface, those words sound logical. But let's stop and reflect on the path that brought us to this moment, and how it now applies to my life. Although I tend to doze in History, I scantily remember a conversation one day about Russian "nesting" dolls. Those little carved wooden things that look like Lenin or Stalin, or some other President on their payroll. The gist is, you pull off their fat, empty, colorful head, and inside is another doll, and then inside that, is *another* doll, and so on and so on and ... zzzzzz. You get the point.

That's the territory we're in now. The morbid equivalent of nesting dolls, figuring that inside a big box ("the van") was another box ("the cargo") that held the urn ("the apartment"), which contains a compact version of William ("the passenger"), who, apparently, once owned the shoebox ("the surprise"). Then, naturally, we were hit by the clown car ("dolt mobile"), which sent us to this fleabag ("the motel"), where something unseen is bound to kill whatever is left of us ("not much"), since our hope died a long time ago.

So what have we learned? Motels are deathtraps. Be sure to label your stuff. And the Russians need to rethink their trinkets.

"Should we open it?" I encourage.

"No!" Dad bristles.

"Why not?"

"It's his private property!" Dad maintains. "He must have wanted it buried with him, so whatever's in there is very important."

"Or it's just shoes," I taunt. "That he *really, really* liked."

Zombie Dad looks at me, blinking. Okay, yeah, that was inane.

"So how does that work?" I give him the third degree. "Do they bury the box next to him? Or just jam all the stuff into his urn?"

"I don't know," Dad admits.

That's disappointing. I was going to use the "jamming" premise to support that we should just save time and do it now.

"What if there's another dead person in the box, and William's trying to get two for the price of one?" I propose. "You owe it to your employer to look."

Either I'm losing my touch, or Zombie Dad has retired for the day.

"No, I'm not doing that," he asserts.

Before I can claim a technicality, he adds, "And neither are YOU."

Wait! How is that fair? I didn't sign any confidentiality paper that says I can't talk about what I see. Sure, theoretically if they sue me, they'll sue Dad because I don't own anything of monetary value that would get anyone excited enough to file court papers. But still, I can't believe that he expects me to just sit idly by, while that box of unknowns dangles in front of me.

"You can't be serious," I huff. "What if there's something illegal in there? Or something dangerous or toxic? Or a severed head?"

Dad tosses me a look, so I concede, "Fine, it's too small for a severed head … unless it's a shrunken voodoo head."

Upon this pronouncement, I decide it may be time to ease up on the conspiracy theories, since I'm truly starting to creep myself out. Face it—mob evidence is one thing, but voodoo stuff is a whole other level of "holy shit, time to hide." So I try to circle back toward the logical … and when a teenager willingly does that, you know things have gotten majorly out of hand.

"You're responsible for my safety, you know. We already got rear-ended today. What if that was no accident? Huh? What if that clown is part of some massive conspiracy of goofballs with bad hair and poor motor skills?"

Dad's trying to blow me off, so I go for the full-court press.

"How much do you even know about William? There could be, like, psycho killers after us, who want whatever's in that box! Didn't you see *Old Country for No Men*? That guy was a *FREAK!!* And what was *up* with that haircut??"

Dad tries to rein in my processor overload. "It's *No Country for Old Men* and since when do you watch R-rated movies?"

"Don't ask questions you don't want the answers to," I scoff.

Dad fixes on me, aghast. So of course, I shift the blame.

"I was babysitting the Callahan kid and he was channel surfing, okay?"

"The Callahan kid doesn't make the rules!" Dad spits.

"Oh yeah? *You* try dealing with him for a night."

Dad sighs, knowing this topic is not worth pursuing. I, however, am not about to let it go. The psycho-killer thing, that is.

"So what if William, like, owed money to gangsters? Goons could bust down the door any second and shoot up the place! And then we'd be swimming with the fishes!"

"It's 'sleeping' with the fishes, and you really should stop watching television," Dad advises.

I give it one last shot.

"It's your duty to open that box and see what you're transporting."

"*NO,*" Dad reprimands. "That's enough. We're not going to talk about it anymore."

As much as parents love the truth, they don't always love it enough to actually want to know it. So killing the conversation is the next best option, and the only hope of keeping things interesting is to throw your own wrench into them.

"Then I'm going shopping," I announce.

Dad stops cold. "Shopping?? Where?"

"There's a Walmart down the street."

"Why do you need to go shopping?" Dad chides.

Aside from the fact that I'm a girl and it's what we do? I couldn't spit out the real reason—that I'm gonna go berserk if I have to look at that shoebox all afternoon. So I make something up.

"I have to buy a battery. For my watch."

Sometimes, Dad shocks me with how observant he is.

"You don't have a watch," he points out.

Damn, I hate when they catch on, because then you just have to dig in deeper.

"Then, I should probably buy one of those, too," I say.

As you can tell, this exchange is not one of my finer moments.

Maybe Dad pities me and my underdeveloped mind, and thinks he failed me since I couldn't come up with something better. Maybe he vaguely remembers dropping me on my head as a kid, which is why I utter daft sentences like that. Or maybe we're descended from a long line of dim bulbs. I'm just speculating, since somebody's to blame for me being a dunce.

"In that case," Dad counters, "I'm going with you."

Whoa, hang on! That wasn't part of the contract. Who threw that little nugget into the mix? I mean, it's mortifying enough to have a parent or anyone that ancient accompany you *anywhere*. But when you're fighting for a few measly scraps of peace and sanity to escape the torture chamber of a non-voluntary road trip, then the gloves just have to come off.

"But ... you can't!" I shriek.

Dad gives me an indignant look, as I reach for the only excuse at hand.

"You have to babysit," I tick my head toward the urn. "He's too little to stay by himself."

"He'll be fine," Dad reasons.

"Are you sure? What if the motel burned down? Or got robbed? You're responsible for getting William to his final resting place. And if something happens, well ... *I smell a lawsuit.*"

Dad knows he can't win this one. Yes, he can dismiss my nutty talk as the blathering of an impatient teenager. But he can't risk losing his one and only job, not after all these months without one. So he caves.

"Then we'll all go," he picks up the urn.

"What??"

"All three of us," Dad smugly boasts, knowing that he's successfully called my bluff. "We're going shopping."

Crud, I didn't see that one coming.

One big happy family, off to Walmart to buy me a watch ... which now destroys my standby excuse for consistently being ten minutes late everywhere. Like I need the added headache of having to be punctual.

I swear that urn is cackling.

"Attention Walmart shoppers ... we have a lost child in the front of the store. Her name is Greer, but she's trying to change that. Her father is here with her, so legally, she hasn't been abandoned. Nevertheless, she has lost her sense of purpose, her sense of humor, her patience, and her last shred of dignity, which jumped ship when their van took it in the shorts from a hungover clown. His lack of coordination has stranded her here for much longer than anyone with standards should have to endure. Not to mention her 'traveling companion' may have mob connections, and the ghoulish

motel clerk is a whole other conversation. Anyone generous enough to rescue her from this apocalyptic joyride and drive her back to Boulder, please come to customer service."

Ah, if only life were as convenient as it is inside my head.

If I hadn't learned at the age of seven that I had crippling stage fright, I would grab that intercom and plead for my safe rescue. But that's nothing more than a pipe dream, ever since a piano recital and a botched version of "Twinkle, Twinkle, Little Star" forever scarred me from the limelight. I still can't readily talk about it, but suffice it to say, a few too many sour notes made the twinkle fizz out prematurely. Even though there was polite applause, I still hear a chorus of boos in my head and shudder at the thought of ever getting in front of an audience again.

As if that humiliation isn't enough for one lifetime, tack onto it that I now have a dead guy in a canister playing party crasher in my backpack. You heard right— it's Dad's bright idea to bring him along, but he makes ME carry him around, to quote, "Be discreet." Really? What if he spills? I'd have human residue coating my textbooks from now 'til graduation. How am I ever supposed to touch them again?

Wait—could that be an excuse for me to drop out of school and never have to go to World History again? If so, it might be worth loosening the hinge. But I can't tamper with anything just yet, since Dad is sticking to me like glue. It never fails ... take a kid out of their normal environment—big city, urban jungle, yadda yadda—and drop them into small-town-middle-of-nowhere, and the parental radar goes off the charts. What? Like I have more chance of getting mugged or kidnapped here? Just because we don't know anybody except for a psycho clown, some jaded mechanics, and two chatty waitresses? They make up at least a quarter of the population. How many more crazies is he expecting to crawl out of the woodwork?

Look, I know he's my dad and all, and yeah I love him, but I gotta ditch this guy for a while. Just a little breather. I need some space.

So I reach for an excuse I watched Liv pull for years—a reason to go to the "lady parts" aisle. She knew that anything involving the thought of his little girl's biological clock being wound up was more than Dad could process, so he routinely avoided that aisle. Since he's now in full-on "protector" mode, I'm not even sure the ploy will work, but my options are running thin.

"I need tampons," I blurt out.

Dad squirms and contorts like a hunchback fending off angry hordes of villagers. "Since when??"

"Since about two years ago."

He looks at me like I'm making this up. Not the part about needing tampons right at the moment—which I am making up, since I've got a couple of weeks lead time before the red army storms the gate. Frankly, he should be grateful, since that's the only thing saving both of us right now. If I had to put up with cramps and bloating on top of all this merriment, somebody would be wearing that urn like a helmet.

But as the wheels turn in Dad's head, I can almost

hear them cranking out his thought process—that maybe I'm making this whole thing up about needing tampons at all, and that I'm not already that old and he hasn't been so checked out that life has largely moved on without him, while Mom has had to pick up the pieces in the major milestones department, since his brain's been off playing in its own backyard bouncy house.

Practically on cue, a little girl walks by with her mother, pushing a doll in a baby stroller. Dad looks longingly at the little girl's angelic image, aching for the days of my vanished youth. He cautiously eyes me like a lab experiment, as if some pigtails and a few props from the toy aisle might turn back time. Hello, kitty.

All I know is, this whole scenario has far too much potential to run off the rails. I gotta move or he's gonna start singing lullabies.

"You don't have to go with me. I know it's dreadful," I emphasize, pretending to do him a favor. "I can just meet you back here."

Traditionally, this is one of those schemes that a parent sniffs out from a mile off, realizing that their kid just wants to avoid them. But Dad's still trying to pull himself together after the whole "toddler on parade" thing. So no alarm bells just yet.

"Um, all right," he mutters. "I'll just, um, be around."

He points to either sporting goods or the vacuum cleaners. I can't tell. To try to dissect his motives would require more energy than I can spare, since he's either high on testosterone or channeling his inner housewife. I don't want to stick around to find out, so I bolt.

Gratefully ducking into the feminine products aisle, I

fight the compulsion to cuddle with the maxi-pads. This must be what prisoners of war feel like once they get back to reality; nothing but love for everything mundane. I get misty-eyed just dipping a toe back into the real world. Ahhhhh, relief. And then ...

Just when I'm starting to come down from this contact high, it happens. A shadowy, fleeting figure pops onto the aisle, intruding on my one and only moment of serenity. Being a bit weepy, I only catch a glance of him out of my peripheral vision, before he takes off. So I'm not a hundred percent on who it is. I would ordinarily assume it must be Dad, playing the overly protective parent. But just from that quick peek, this guy was too short to be Dad, who's probably still wandering around, trying to find my lost childhood. Plus, whoever it was, they had on one of those puffy wintery jackets with a hood, which was pulled up around their face. So technically, I can't even be sure it was a *he*. But it must have been, since no woman on a shopping excursion would ever wear a puffy jacket that could inhibit a quick mirror-check of impulse purchases from the sale rack. We need to grab, glimpse, and go. Time is money, and no one understands that better than a woman with a credit card.

So, yeah—it was a guy. A miniature guy, but still a guy.

At first, I'm relieved that I'm just getting an ounce of space. But then I start obsessing about why a guy would step onto the douche aisle, and then flake as soon as I look in his direction. Was he confused? Possibly. Was he sent on the obligatory errand to pick up tampons for his wife and just too embarrassed to grab the goods while someone else was around? Potentially. But if that's the case, he better learn to be a team player pretty quick, considering that no husband wants to return home empty-handed to a PMS'ing wife with a critical shopping list.

Maybe it was some amped-up pre-teen who got kicked out of the bra department for too much window shopping, since he's not old enough to buy dirty magazines. So now he's seeing if there's any lewd packaging to explore among the panty liners. But then it registers with me ...

He took off pretty fast. Like, *wayyyy* faster than most guys would have dared, given the sight of an alluring ingénue amongst the feminine décor. They couldn't get that many beguiling visitors in this place, so you'd think he would have hovered a few more seconds, to enjoy the rapture. But he ran away before I even got a real look at him. Which can only mean ...

I have a stalker. Which, under normal circumstances, could be glibly written off, since high schoolers readily tend to find each other fascinating on a short-term basis. But ...

We're in a rinky-dink town, where I don't know anybody. And for a stalker to have followed me from Boulder and trade in their spring break for this road trip from hell is beyond stretching the bounds of credibility, since teenage obsession tends to end whenever we have to do actual work ... not to mention use our own gas money. So the stalking theory doesn't quite hold up, unless you take into account ...

I'm carrying around a dead guy.

Not only that—I'm carrying around a dead guy who

prepaid for strangers to transport him out of state. Which is quirky enough, if it just ended there. But *noooooo* ...

I'm carrying around a dead guy who prepaid for strangers to transport him out of state, along with a mysterious shoebox that might as well be ticking, because who knows what the heck is in it since Dad's playing puritan and refuses to interfere in other people's business, even though it's perfectly acceptable to demand that I lug around ash in my backpack, but when it comes to fact-checking the cargo, suddenly it's all about "boundaries," which is really just a flowery term for "laziness," since it would take too much work to lift a lid to see what we're up against, and good luck trying to find out what the deductible is on Digby's insurance and whether it covers any "accidents" (wink, wink) that may arise because of shady clients, so we'll just keep our blissful distance and pretend that all's right with the world while we're basically sitting ducks at that hovel of a motel where big-bellied Walter probably has a mummified relative or two in the attic, which is all the more reason why I'm spooning with sanitary napkins, which can only mean ...

We're being followed by the mob.

I immediately whip out my phone and hit speed dial.

"Where are you?" Liv hears the panic in my voice.

"In a Walmart in farm country."

"You're in the suburbs?"

"No! REAL farm country!" I stress. "Like cows and dust bowls, and clowns and tumbleweeds."

"Why would you go there?" Liv recoils.

"Don't you remember the whole road trip thing we discussed when I was packing?"

"Sort of, but I was only half-listening," Liv admits.

Truthfully, I don't even know why I expect more. But since my life could be in imminent danger, it's worth a shot.

"Well pay attention now, because the cops may need to trace this phone call."

I quickly run down the condensed version of this bad reality show that is now my life, and beg Liv to rescue me. Finally, she catches on.

"Wait, this is that whole 'dead guy' thing? *That's* why you're ... wherever? Okay, now it's coming back to me."

At this point, I can't even tell if this conversation is worth depleting my cell phone battery, considering I may need it for shock therapy. Despite "phoning a friend," I may have to rethink my move and go straight for my lifeline, which means Liv's my only hope of getting out of here intact.

"Now I have to go to a rodeo," I elaborate, "because some clown got baked and couldn't just pay us off with real money."

Liv cringes at both prospects. "Rodeos and clowns? Ick!"

Realizing that I may have struck a nerve, I go for the big finish.

"And I think the mafia is following us."

That's got to be enough to sell the urgency. In a normal family, anyway.

"Relax," Liv says, nonchalant. "They've been tailing Uncle Barney for years, and he's still got his thumbs. Don't be so paranoid."

I knew this would take a bad turn. But I'm not about

to let Uncle Barney's misguided affinity for gambling and support hose (don't ask) ruin my shot at freedom. So I toss one last Hail Mary, and like most desperate passes, it's a stretch.

"I've got nine dollars, a Starbuck's card and my iPod," I offer. "I'll give you everything. *Just get me outta here!!*"

"Hang on," Liv fires back. "I can't just drop everything and drive to wherever. I have my own crisis going on right now. Remember??"

The "baby" card? Again? Look, I get that it's a major life issue and all, but give me a break. I'm clinging to a ledge here. What about me? What about the dramas of my life, which are growing more consuming by the second? But since I'm a giver, I try to be supportive.

"How's that going? Did you tell Mom?"

"No!" Liv barks. "Why? Did you tell Dad??"

"No! He's on enough trips right now."

"Which is another reason I can't come and get you," Liv contends.

I brace myself for what's bound to be a colorful explanation. Although, you never fully realize how much dirty laundry there is in your family, until someone explores the hamper. Liv's already trotted out Uncle Barney. What else is lingering at the bottom?

"Dad's still hanging by a thread," she claims. "Right?"

I peek around the edge of the aisle and catch a glimpse of him in sporting goods.

"He's looking at fishing poles," I report.

"Why?" Liv squawks. "Dad doesn't fish. Does he?"

"I don't think so. But I'm not, like, joined at the hip with him twenty-four hours a day. He may have hobbies."

Now he's studying the archery bows. What? Is he planning to go off the grid and hunt his own food?

"That's probably how the 'Unabomber' started," Liv presumes, having no idea if that's even remotely true. "He had a meltdown and lived in the woods, which Dad could be planning if he's looking at survival gear, which means Mom's gonna flip if you abandon him."

Abandon? Does she have to use such a harsh word? It's not like I'm never gonna see him again. I mean, he'll come home eventually, right? They might sell maps here. I could get him a pocket version. Besides, I don't think people "plan" meltdowns. That sounds like a more spontaneous thing. Case in point ...

"And don't even get me started on Mom," Liv drones on, "who's in such a tizzy with this whole wedding thing, I can barely deal. So you should be glad you're with the *less* crazy parent, since Mom's ready to lose it on that bride, who's beyond lucky I'm not there, since I would have clocked that bitch by now."

Why me, Lord? I just want a ride. A simple "Point A to Point B" trajectory. Why is it so much to ask? It's not out of the realm of comprehension. It happens every day. People get into their cars, and they go somewhere. Then they get back into their cars, and they return to wherever they started. Simple math. But for some reason, in my family, it's an impossible equation.

True, I could just take the van keys and peel off in a moment of reckless abandon. But that's *so* not cool, since there's probably no cab service here, and a prolonged bus trip could make even the most stable person lose their marbles. I can't do that to Dad, no matter how excruciating this whole thing is. Not to mention, there's also the little matter of the "little matter" in my backpack.

"He's making you carry that thing around??" Liv reacts, horrified.

"Well, it's not like we can parade it everywhere," I grant. "Although, I did whip it out at lunch, which was pretty funny." Damn, I should have taken a picture.

Seeing as I've already tried bribes and demands, I have a go at one last angle for rescue: pity.

"I just want to come home," I beg. "Please??"

"Look, I get that this blows," Liv says. "And I don't blame you for wanting to bail. But he's our dad. And yeah, he's kind of a head case right now, but he needs you."

I can't believe this. Of all people, Liv is being the voice of reason.

"Think of it as a role reversal thing," she continues. "You're responsible for *him*."

Already? Not that it's a total shock. I know from when my grandma lived with us that, at some point, the kids become the parents and the parents become the kids. It's sorta like having overgrown toddlers, where you have to keep them from burning the house down, in-between some babbling and occasional bedwetting. I just didn't expect it to be happening so soon. Maybe Liv has a heightened sense of these things, now that she's facing parenthood of her own. Maybe she's magically grown up a bit.

Or not.

"Besides, I have a hair appointment tomorrow," she adds. "And my roots are in dire need of attention."

Go ahead, say it—I looked too deeply into the face of hope and was sternly dismissed. *"Nothing to see here people. Move along."*

As I hang up, I stare at the happy faces of the women on the douche boxes, and longingly wonder, "Where do these people live, and how do I get there??"

10

LAST NAMES

DAY TWO (Part Three):
The Merciless Stampede of Tuesday.

"Do we really have to go to a rodeo tonight? Can't we just blow it off and watch TV?"

"That would be rude," Dad emphasizes.

"No, I'd say ramming our van and trapping us here is significantly more rude," I charge.

"It was an accident."

"You sure about that? A mysterious clown just happens to pop up out of nowhere? He could be a highly paid, badly dressed hit man, and this could all be part of a grander plan. One that we're only scratching the surface of. That's why I'm in the 'mafia chair,' casing the door. You'd be smart to do the same, because once I duck, I may or may not be able to save you."

After the boundless fun of our shopping binge, Dad and I now sit in the café part of Walmart, drinking sodas (or "pops" as they're known here) and pontificating the warning signs of hysteria.

"Your conspiracy theories need to take a day off," Dad advises.

I stare at him in grim silence, determined to shame him into action. Giving in, he inches his chair around to keep one eye peeled on the main doors. For appearances, he's only doing it to shut me up. But I can see the paranoia slowly starting to creep in, feeding on his brain. It's all starting to add up to one big, convoluted game, in which we are merely pawns.

My eyes search every corner of the ceiling.

"What are you doing?" Dad asks.

"Looking for hidden cameras," I say. "They're bound to be watching. We could be on TV right now, and the whole world could be watching."

"This isn't *The Truman Show*. We're not that popular."

"What channel is that on?"

"Never mind," Dad sighs, not wanting to feed the beast of my suspicions.

So we sit here, killing time. Dad won't fess up, but he's just as wiped as I am. Then he starts to scratch. No, not one of those horribly embarrassing "Dad" scratches— you know the ones, when they're sitting on the couch and think no one but the dog is looking. And since dogs recognize the need to address one's crotch, it's just naturally assumed that there'll be no degree of insult.

No, this is the "I may have athlete's foot" scratch, where he's rubbing his shoes together, because it would make too much sense to take off his shoe to properly resolve the issue. Yes, I know we're in public, but this day can't get any more humiliating, so why bother being a slave to decorum?

"My foot itches," Dad winces.

"You don't say," I scowl.

"I think I'll get some foot powder while we're here."
Dad gets up, halfway expecting me to follow.

"Do I have to come, too?" I grimace.

He throws me the type of look that's readily exchanged between traveling companions who've grown tired of each other while stuck in a third-world country. The discomfited slant of the brow after incessant bickering about which one is going to have to go back into the fish market and haggle, while the other contemplates ditching them on anything with wheels or hooves. Oh yeah—he knows what he's up against.

"I guess not," he says. "As long as you promise to stay right here."

I don't understand his somewhat pissy stance, since I'm ultimately doing him a favor. I know full well he's too embarrassed to have me tag along when buying foot powder, since that aisle could include stuff for jock itch and any number of other annoyances of the male species. But seeing as he's my legal guardian du jour, he has to make some kind of overture to supervise my welfare so that I don't make an offhand comment to Mom that will have him getting an earful about lax parenting skills for the next few decades.

Or maybe he overheard my conversation with Liv—although, I doubt it, since that fishing pole threw him for a pretty long loop. Maybe he suspects that a getaway plan has been hatched, and now needs to be quashed. Or maybe all my talk of conspiracy theories has made him truly paranoid.

NOTE TO SELF: Conspiracy theories only work if people immediately buy into them. They have an expiration date, so if left to fester, can sprout in unwanted directions. Tend your garden wisely.

The only remedy here is to quickly challenge my rival, making him show his cards.

"Where else am I gonna go?" I lament.

Remember when I said that Dad sometimes shocks me with how much he's actually paying attention? This also goes for the unexpected maneuver of turning the tables on me in the bullshit department.

"Wherever it is," Dad whispers, "they'll know. They may be listening."

He draws a finger to his mouth in a "ssshhh" gesture. His eyes drift up toward the ceiling—suspiciously looking for the imaginary cameras I was touting in a feeble attempt to keep myself entertained. Boy, did that ploy go south.

Dad inches away, pretending to flinch at every sound and sudden movement. It's bad enough when parents succeed in calling out your nonsense, but when they play along, then it's simply not funny anymore. Which is probably by design, but really ... must we *all* act like children?

As Dad skirts toward the male itch aisle, I sit in the café, bitterly mulling over my lot in life. Other people my age are enjoying their spring break right now, reveling in the mindless abandon of being a teenager. But I'm stuck in Bumfrick Egypt because of some ridiculous provision in a guy's will, which set in motion this uncoordinated square dance between a beater van, a spiteful clown, and two needy traveling companions—one who is getting foot powder, and one who *is* foot powder. It's like the butterfly effect, after fate maims it with a flyswatter.

So, I sit. Alone. Tapping my fingers on the table.

Tap, tap, tap ... a rhythmic grind, playing out the aching wail in my head. No one else could possibly know my pain. Could they?

TAP, TAP, TAP ...

Just so you know, *that's not me*. Oh, it's a real sound, all right. But it's coming from somewhere else. Could it be that the universe has heard my cries and is throwing me a lifeline? That somewhere in this café, amidst scattered hot dog wrappers and airborne grease embedded in sticky Formica, there could be an escape hatch to save me from this mind warp? It's like a call of the wild, singing to me. I don't know how else to describe it.

"Morse code?" a voice wonders aloud.

Whoa. Is the universe literally talking to me? Have we teleported beyond the ethereal into another realm? I know it's a thing, but I'm so not ready to live on Mars yet.

"You're doing Morse code, right?" the voice emerges again.

Sheez, the universe is rather pushy. When it wants answers, you better hop to it. As for me, I more or less crawl.

"Huh?" I look around.

"Pssst," the voice calls. "Over here."

TAP, TAP, TAP ...

From a booth in the corner comes the beckoning sound. I look over, anxiously searching for the white knight that has come to rescue me. The strapping hero on a great stallion, like the covers of those steamy novels I used to find tucked among Grandma's crossword puzzles.

Alas, emerging from the tempest that has inhaled the tatters of my spring break is the stunning vision of ...

A nerd.

"Hey," he smiles, flashing more metal than one of the clown's hair bands. "It's not often you meet someone who knows Morse code."

"I don't know it," I say. "I'm just bored."

"Wow," the nerd marvels. "Your technique sounds fairly proficient."

It figures. I'm a virtuoso of boredom, and this trip has unleashed the prodigy within me.

"If we were on a submarine right now, you might even launch an international incident," the geek laughs, letting out a snort.

And we're off! Just when I think this trip can't get any more bizarre, a bout of dork humor rears its nearsighted head. But wait, there's more!

"You might have skills that you're not even aware of," he suggests. "You could have learned them in past lives, but have suppressed them."

"This life's a major handful as it is," I determine. "My plate's pretty full."

"I'm just underscoring a point. Anything is possible."

And then, as if to prove that point, I notice ...

There's something almost familiar about this nerd. I can't quite put my finger on it. Maybe it's the way he slaps his tongue against his braces to make that annoying "hissing" sound when he talks. Or maybe it's the weak stab at a faux Mohawk, even though his hair's too short to even hope for baby bangs. Like most geeks, there's the dual sensation of a person trying too hard to fit in, coexisting with a person who has just socially given up.

That's it!! *Coexisting!* As in my earlier observation—"*he just never seemed to grasp the whole concept of coexisting, in general.*" Shut the front door!! Can it be??

"*Linus??*" I gape at him. "Linus Beadleman?"

"Who's that?" he plays dumb.

"*You??*"

"Me??"

"You went to my junior high? In Boulder?"

"No," he says unconvincingly.

"Yes you did," I contend. "You had, um ... reddish hair? And glasses? Or, wait – was your hair more brown?"

He stares at me, offended.

"You claim you knew this guy, but you don't remember what he looked like?"

"Well, I kinda do. But ... you know, it was a while ago, and I've never been one for details," I confess.

"So you have ADD?"

"No, I just don't pay much attention to things," I grant. "But it *is* you, right? You can tell me."

"What's that supposed to mean?"

I elaborate on how the common wisdom was hedging bets on whether Linus had a sex change or joined a cult.

"Although I never bought into the sex change idea," I haughtily profess. "Even our Australian exchange student said it sounded like a 'bit of a furphy'."

Linus stares at me like a deer in headlights. He's not even being coy—it's more like dead silence. Such a reaction might normally make me question my conclusion. But seeing as Vera Fernlander was still bouncing through the halls as of last week, it's not realistic that Linus is living a double-life, since the commute from here would be beyond tedious. So it must be the cult thing, which was my theory to begin with, thank you very much. Although, this commune must be pretty underground, since he still has a semi-normal haircut and no sign of a tambourine.

"So which cult is it?" I inquire. "One of those where you channel aliens while you wait for the apocalypse? Or do you just go to 'Burning Man' and chant? Hey, did your parents have to sign some sort of brainwashing release?"

Not that I'm looking to join. I just want the particulars for when I stick it to everyone who thought I was wrong.

"Look, I'm not this 'Linus' guy, whoever you're talking about," he says.

"I get it," I offer, trying to play along. "The cult gave you a new name, which would be …?"

"My name is Hugh."

Hugh? Wow, I would have expected more. Like something with a few more syllables and some numbers.

"That's the best they could come up with?" I frown.

He shoots me a look. "Oh yeah? What's your name?"

Now I've stepped in it. I keep telling myself to exercise restraint in the name-calling department, since I have no recourse. But as usual, I ignore etiquette and pay the price when it backfires.

"You really have to go there, Linus?" I spitefully retort. "I don't remember you being so cold."

"I just asked your name. How is that cold?"

Linus naively views this interaction as a polite exchange, so I try to give him some leeway, as I answer through clenched teeth, "Greer."

Linus's eyes dart about, running through a Rolodex in his head.

"And your last name?"

"Sarazen."

He shakes his head. "Doesn't ring a bell."

How rude. At least I faintly remember him. The fact that Linus doesn't remember me is beyond shocking. Not that I'm the most popular girl in school, but I'm not wallpaper, either. He's gotta be faking it.

"Linus, you can give up the charade. The cult people aren't here." I look around, paranoid. "Are they?"

"I told you, my name is Hugh," he insists. "And I'm not in a cult."

His persistent tone would indicate that he mysteriously believes this, which could be the result of successful mind bending. Or, perhaps, an even more devious scheme . . .

"Ohhhh, now I get it," I nod. "Witness protection program."

This is fascinating; so far beyond the scope of what I envisioned for young Linus. To be among the rare few who openly testify against people so ruthless that you have to go into hiding . . . and *change your name.*

"How does that work?" I brighten up. "Do you actually have to be involved in something illegal or can you just get an application online?"

"I don't know. I'm not in witness protection."

"C'mon, Linus," I prod. "You can tell me. You're among friends."

"Not really. You barely remember this guy."

He has a point, but I can't let him know that.

"Give me a break," I huff. "It was two years ago. You

could have grown five inches and developed facial hair in that time."

True or not, Linus buys that excuse for the moment. It is pretty pathetic that I can't remember more about a guy who has oddly inhabited a corner of my brain for a while now. Is it possible that I'm just projecting onto the nearest warm body to satisfy my own curiosity? Or maybe I'm so utterly bored that my mind has invented someone to keep me occupied. Is this how multiple personalities start? Is Linus even real? Should I throw something at him, to see if he flinches? Before the melee can start, he launches the first strike.

"If you're from Boulder, why are you here?" he picks at the scab of my existence.

I relay the condensed version of the story, since the whole soap opera would take way too long to unfold, and who knows when Dad's going to emerge from the personal disinfectant aisle.

"So you're carrying around an actual dead person?" Linus asks, intrigued.

I allow him to peek into my backpack, since Dad gets funny about parading our guest around.

"How'd he die?"

"You got me," I shrug. "Dad's holding the paperwork hostage."

"You need to find out," Linus demands. "Knowing his story will enrich your days together."

Hang on—that thought process screams of familiarity.

"Were you tight with the Buddha?" I ask. "Because that sounds like something he would say."

"Buddha?"

"Greer?" Dad joins in.

"Dad?"

"Who …?" he points to the geek.

"Linus," I respond.

"Hugh," the nerd interjects.

"Me?" Dad hears him wrong.

"No, Hugh."

"Huh?" Dad squints.

"This is Linus," I claim.

"No, I'm not," the nerd maintains.

"I went to school with him."

"No you didn't," the nerd protests.

"Huh?" Dad repeats.

"*Hugh,*" the nerd insists.

"Oy," I sigh.

Dad shakes it off, not wanting to delve too deep. Mostly, he's just relieved that I'm still here, which must be why he doesn't seem worried about me talking to weirdos. Or it's the obvious truth that I could snap Linus like a twig, since he's not exactly beefy.

Dad wastes no time in prodding me to go. He's tired and wants to rest up for our big night at the rodeo.

"A disco nap?" Linus lights up.

Dad tosses him a befuddled look.

"How do you know that term?"

"I'm particularly fascinated by that period of the late '70s to early '80s," Linus proudly announces. "The outgrowth of esoteric dance amidst world strife and the looming resurgence of the Cold War is quite a cultural dichotomy, wouldn't you say?"

Dad just blinks.

"I'm not disparaging it," Linus elaborates, which doesn't necessarily help, since neither of us knows what he's talking about. "I'm quite taken with the whole disco movement. You should try it sometime."

"What?" Dad asks, baffled.

"Disco dancing. It's quite a release."

Dad can't dignify that with a response, and turns to me. "We should leave."

"Town??" I quickly come back to life.

"No, the store."

"Maybe I'll see you at the barrel race," Linus bubbles with all the anxious fervor that comes from shockingly having a social calendar.

Oh yippy—the rodeo is the hot ticket. How lucky we are to know the clown bouncer manning the velvet rope, so we can show up fashionably late. I fight the urge to race back to the maxi-pads for some last-minute spooning, but know it's only a temporary fix. Might as well just saddle up and get it over with.

As for Linus, I would say he didn't use to be like this, but I don't remember. Was he into disco and politics? Are those regarded as strange bedfellows when they don't involve dollar bills and lap dances? And what the frick color was his hair? It's bugging me now.

Just as Dad and I head for the exit, reality finds a new way to sideline us, when William's mobile home sends the alarm bells into a frenzy. The security guard and store manager examine the urn like a bewildered tag team, uneasy about what mayhem has landed in their once quiet town. Before Dad can explain, an overzealous clerk grabs the store intercom.

"Gardenware, please send an associate to the front."
Bring some fertilizer, too. I don't have enough crap to
deal with.

*

I knew I'd get screwed on this grand bargain. I should
have picked the Bridezilla. No matter how Liv describes
Mom's current state of mind, a stuck-up society wedding
has to be better than the dusty Shangri-La where I now
wile away my days. Attitude, schmattitude. At least they'd
have cake. Probably damn good cake. But, no. I get
donuts with sprinkles, and that's only if Walter's in a
mood to share. Given that I'm about the circumference
of his belly button, I'd bet it's a losing battle.

Looking around our sad little motel room, it's obvious
I need to write a snippy letter to my travel agent. But my
travel agent is now getting his beauty sleep for a rodeo,
while I babysit little William. I stare at Dad while he naps,
and debate if he's truly tired, or if he's just thrown in the
towel. As usual, I've once again drawn the short straw
and had to become the responsible party. That's a big pair
of shoes to fill, you know. And just like that ...

DING, DING, DING!!! We have a winner! As in ...
shoes?? Or should I say, "*Snooping, anyone??*"

You ever have one of those moments when fate not
only throws you a bone, but throws you a buffet? Such an
unexpected surprise, you halfway expect that you've
either just been punked or have been sleepwalking and
are gonna wake up naked in your neighbor's birdbath? I
swear, I'd start weeping if it wouldn't waste time.

This little scenario could turn out to be HUGE if a certain parent stays asleep long enough, considering that a certain shoebox has been designated off-limits while said parent has been awake. But no disclaimer was made about "if I happen to nod off," so as the responsible party in the room, I think it's my duty to know the full scope of our situation. With my co-pilot out of it, I feel it would be smart to read the manual in the meantime, in case we need to make an emergency landing.

That's my story and I'm sticking to it.

Luckily, the room is cramped enough that there aren't tons of hiding places, so the box isn't hard to find. Then again, the room is cramped enough that there aren't tons of hiding places if the sleeping giant awakes. Sadly, the penthouse suite wasn't an option in this dump, so here we are. Then again, there is no penthouse suite in this dump, so we both know that I'm throwing in this anecdote mainly just to gripe.

I tiptoe to the corner of the room and hunker down with the shoebox. My fingers gently start to lift the lid when—

Dad grunts. Not quite a snore, but more like one of those inelegant "Dad" emissions—a cross between a belch and a wheeze. Such hubbubs usually happen after too much junk food, so he may have downed some Walmart nachos when I wasn't looking. Let's hope not, since that would make this the first passage in a symphony of clumsy noises to come.

I start to open the box again, when more commotion arises from Dadland. Only this time, it includes the peculiar "mumbling" that often surfaces in-between stanzas in dreamland. Hopefully, he's not in a mood to ramble, since—I don't know about you—but I'm getting pretty friggin' tired of the intrusions. Unless ...

In the worst-case scenario, Dad is truly awake and is trying to psyche me out, which he knows will make me crazier than just loudly telling me to put the box down. Historically, Mom is more inclined to such head games, which she chalks up to the parenting method of giving me the opportunity to recognize my error and willingly change my ways, before I invariably ignore my conscience and get busted, regardless. Who knows which game plan is at work here, since it would involve looking over at Dad, who's either conked out or smirking. So I employ the tried and true childhood method of holding my breath and staying perfectly still while pretending to be invisible, since nothing could possibly go wrong with that idea.

Dad rolls over, which means that either he's still sleeping or just doesn't care anymore. Or maybe I really am invisible—which would be the most amazingly spectacular thing ever and absolutely surpass anything in this box. But until that answer can be sorted out, let's proceed.

I start on the lid again. This whole thing is so off the charts, I can barely stand it. For once, what I'm doing on my spring break may *finally* be more exciting than whatever my friends are doing. Think about it—what if there genuinely is something illegal or scandalous inside this box? Stolen property or incriminating evidence that could irrevocably change lives, assuming the mob doesn't "off" us first. If it's important enough to want to bury it, perhaps it wasn't meant for prying eyes. All the more reason to open it. At long last, the one shred of excitement to be had this entire week, and Dad's sleeping through it. Classic.

Here we go ... opening. And, we haaaaave ...

A foot.

No, not like a severed horror movie foot. Please. Aside from long-term nightmares, the sheer intrigue of that would have me beyond jazzed. But, no. What I get is nowhere near that exciting. Why, you ask? Because it's made of wood. Yes, you heard me. A wooden foot. Or rather, it's more like the shape of a foot, since there aren't toes or anything too descript. Just a honking piece of wood, shaped like a foot. Can't see any gangsters chasing us down over this. *Unless* ...

It *is* an actual foot, just encased in wood. Can they do that? Put a "wood coating" on a foot? It's not that far out, right? After all, you can cover things in chocolate, plastic, fiberglass. Why not wood? Or, or, OR ...

What if there's, like, a giant wad of cash stuffed in the wooden foot? Like a nest egg of marked bills, only instead of an egg, it's a nest foot? You know, like one of those "hide a key" things you put in your yard and pretend it's a lawn ornament, then just hope no burglars are bright enough to catch on. Maybe this is a "hide a stolen loot" thing, shaped like a foot. Nobody would think to look there ... unless I just blew that theory. But it could happen. Couldn't it??

Standby, there's more. Not feet. Just—are you kidding me? *Another* box, about the size of my hand, with painted words on the front and back: "Bee" and "Live." Whaaa?

Seriously, this box mania is out of control. And why so cryptic? Did he have a thing for bees? The words look like they were painted by hand. Ooh! Maybe he died of a bee sting and in his last breath he was trying to identify the killer with a bloody scrawl. Except he keeled over before he could add "flying" and "fuzzy." It happens all the time on TV, right? But since the box has a tiny padlock and I don't carry around a tiny crowbar, looks like we're all gonna remain clueless.

Last item up...there's a picture. A snapshot of a baby wrapped in a blanket, with the hands of a man and a woman each cradling the infant's body. The baby seems normal ... although it's wrapped up pretty good, sleeping, so I can't tell if it's an alien. I don't see antennas or anything, but that could be the reason for all the wrapping. It's not like you want to advertise it if your kid fell off the mother ship and missed the train to Roswell.

That's it. Nothing else in the box. All this hoopla for three things: a photo, a little box, and a wooden foot. I dared to get excited over this? They obviously meant something to William. But what's the point of burying these things? The picture —okay, I get that, since pictures can be sentimental. But it boggles the mind what the box is. Maybe he had a thing for bees. But what's up with the wooden foot? Help me out here. Of all the things you could choose to bury with you—*WHY A WOODEN FOOT?* If he had a shoe obsession, I'm sure there were any number of cute footwear choices that he could have packed up to take with him, which—c'mon now—we'd all do, if we could, right?

I suppose the fact that the foot's wooden means that it

would last longer than a real one, assuming the termites don't catch on. So it's an inspired way to keep up with a foot fetish, I'll give him that. But still ... I don't get it.

Dad's snoring, so he's checked out. Or he's faking it. Nothing shocks me anymore. Snoring is a trip. How anyone can be that noisy and that out of it at the same time is beyond me. But at least I know he's alive without having to walk over there and check. So it is a time-saver.

I wonder if William snored—if he, too, sounded like an idling buzz saw. And if he did that, what else did he do when he was alive? Looking at these things now—the picture, especially—I'm reminded that, yes, he *was* alive. I mean, sure, I knew that already. But I didn't really think about his actual life. What he looked like or how he spent his time. Did he have a wife or kids? What music did he listen to? Was he popular? That's a silly question, I guess. What does that even mean, to be a "popular" adult? I'm not talking famous people; I'm talking average people. Once you're out of high school, how do you gauge if you're popular? Your number of online friends? If you get a promotion? Or how many people show up at your funeral?

I stare at the urn and, for the first time, start to genuinely regard the man inside. The man he used to be.

Since William prearranged this little tour, it must have occurred to him at some point that an outsider would probably be transporting him. Somebody who wouldn't have known him, and wouldn't have cared, beyond the job that they were hired to do. Is that what he wanted? Somebody detached?

Or was he hoping it would be a friend?

11

LAST ROUNDUP

DAY TWO (Part Four):
The Endless Mutha Effin' Time Warp of Tuesday.

"This town ain't big enough for the three of us."

I thought in every Western there were gangs of outlaws waiting to run people out of town. Or it's the sheriff trying to run off the outlaws. No matter what, there's always somebody who's pissed that somebody else is there, and wants them to leave. That's more or less the storyline.

Believe me, I'm more than happy to play along. I wouldn't even put up a fight. No need to draw pistols. I come and go in peace, even if I don't speak the language. Me just want van back.

If only I were a horse thief, this rodeo thing would come in handy. But, no. I never bothered to learn horse thieving, or any other cowboy traits that could serve me now. All those years of scoffing at the optional "Dude Ranch" excursion over summer break have officially come back to haunt me. I pompously thought, "Why would I ever want or need hog-tying skills? What a waste of my precious time." Now my mind runs amok with the "what ifs" of mislaid opportunity. What if I did know how to steal a horse and could ride off into the sunset before anyone noticed? What if I could strap the clown like a pair of antlers to the front of the van, so for once, he'd see where he was going? What if I could hog-tie Walter just for the sheer amusement of it (assuming I could find enough rope)?

Sadly, such entertainment is only in my head. Reality is not nearly as obliging. Need proof? Try this ten-gallon on for size: Dad's looking at cowboy hats. Oh Lord. It's bad enough to be mingling with the locals. We don't need to start looking the part. He's at a booth that seemingly sells every dimension and style known to man. They even have a little "steamer" thing to shape the brim, so you can virtually meld it to your head. Like there's no distinction between where your skull ends and the cowboy hat begins. Your head is just one big, continuous hat. Speaking of mind melds ...

"You made it!" Linus moseys on up.

Ah yes, the cult's resident personality.

"Hi Linus."

"It's Hugh," he insists.

Here we go again. If I could just make him understand that denial about one's name only works for so long, it could at least be a gentler fall. Although I give him credit for his manic dedication, it's time to talk him down.

"Even if you've convinced yourself of that, you don't look like a Hugh," I declare. "Can't they can assign you a better name?"

"Who? My parents?"

"No, that's a lost cause," I advise. "Trust me—they'll

push back, just because they can. Talk to your Swami or whoever is in charge of the day-to-day cult stuff. They could likely pull a few strings."

Considering that Linus is much brighter than most teenagers, he quickly wakes up to the realization that he's in a losing battle and changes the subject.

"So is this your first rodeo?" he cheerily asks.

"Mmm hmm. Big day for me."

"Being from Colorado, I would have thought you'd been to a rodeo, before," Linus theorizes.

It strikes me that Linus is trying to pull a fast one.

"Wait, you're from Colorado, too," I remind him. "Didn't you ever go to one of these things?"

"I've never been to Colorado," Linus asserts.

"Oh, Linus," I sigh. "Those de-programmers really did a number on you. You're like a clean slate."

Actually, that's kind of inviting. Just think of how appealing it could be to simply start over at times, and pretend that certain years never happened. Currently, my vote would be for seventh grade, since that was the height of my obligatory "ugly phase"—that pimple-ridden, buck-toothed chain gang every tween must ride out. I tried to burn that school picture, but Mom had a conniption. We reached a truce when she allowed me to do some Photoshop to it, but that quickly backfired once I was forced to accept that I didn't remotely look like the supermodel I'd created, and it became such a bore when people kept asking, "Who's that?" So it was back to reality, with a few zit touch-ups. The only good thing about the "ugly phase"—you have nowhere to go but up.

Fittingly, my inner dialogue has now preoccupied me

long enough for Linus to change the subject again. Or he's just ignoring me and moving on.

"So did you bring your friend?" Linus points to my backpack. "You know ... the urn?"

"Yeah, he's here. We're pretty much inseparable at this point."

"Must be confounding," Linus supposes, "to be responsible for someone you didn't even know."

I dwell on that idea, realizing—

"I sorta know him. A little."

Before Linus can start grilling me, Dad comes over. Thankfully, without a cowboy hat.

"Hello again, sir," Linus kisses ass.

"You remember Linus?" I prompt Dad.

"My name is Hugh," Linus reiterates.

"You sure about that?" I needle him.

Linus flits me a weary glance, while Dad has given up on the name game.

"Hello ... young man," Dad mumbles.

"I'm so glad you could attend tonight," Linus boasts. "And just so you know, my neighbor works the fried butter stand. In case you want some."

If anything ever deserved a vacant look, it has to be that statement.

"Is that an actual menu choice?" Dad asks, perplexed.

"That's the whole menu," Linus concedes.

In an effort to bring refinement to the cuisine at county fairs, it seems that a snobbish food collective developed the discerning option of "fried butter," which is beyond wrong on so many levels. In essence, it's a deep-fried stick of butter, on a stick. A compact snack aimed at those who freely throw caution to the wind and their cholesterol into turmoil. In light of my general attention span, I only hazily remember the food pyramid. But I'm pretty certain fried butter was nowhere on it.

"No thanks, we're saving room," I say. "Tomorrow is sprinkles day."

Dad pretends to be enthused, then takes my arm, coaxing, "We should get our seats."

An awkward silence, as Linus lingers in the uncomfortable void of being a third wheel. Or, in this case, he's more like a sidecar, since the third wheel is in my backpack. And since the clown will probably show up on a unicycle, he'd be a separate vehicle.

Moments like this are never easy and require either brutal honesty or the deft touch of a social surgeon who can cleanly cut ties. Public severing is a skill I have yet to fully master, and as much as Dad might secretly want to be a prick at times, he can't seem to drum up the final dose of jerkwad required.

"Would you like to join us?" he invites Linus, all the while clutching my arm in the hopes of rendering me silent.

"I'd love to!" Linus beams.

Under normal circumstances, I would interject at this point and level a verbal death knell. But even I can't bring myself to kill Linus's surging confidence. Considering that his usual locale is a lonely booth at the Walmart café, an evening of parading around a casual acquaintance with big-city folk is bound to earn him a few points on the sliding scale of popularity. So off we go, into the wild blue arena.

"It's very dusty," I feign a cough for maximum effect. Then, like a spine-chilling Jackass in the Box—

"Hey! You made it!"

The clown pops up, as I scream and hide in Dad's jacket.

"Oh, sorry, dude. Didn't mean to scare you."

Really? In case you haven't noticed, you're a friggin' clown! You people are terrifying.

"Wasn't sure you'd show, after that whole deal today," he grovels.

How dare he—a *deal?* The trauma of this unwelcome detour had me taking a clingy vacation on the tampon aisle, and he has the nerve to call it a deal? No, a deal is something that's agreed upon, by all parties. Let's get something straight—I didn't sign up for this, *dude.* I was bullied into a losing proposition, and now it's just a fight for survival, which is the only thing keeping me away from the fried butter.

The clown then dials up the psychosis.

"Oh man, I should have offered you a ride, since you don't have a car."

As if I'd ever set foot in that death machine. I've already been a crash test dummy once today.

"Don't worry about it, we're fine," Dad tries to be polite.

The clown elects to play tour guide, pointing out the best seats, because who wouldn't want a bird's eye view of someone getting gored?

"It's my job to distract the bull," the clown brags. "In case things get outta hand."

You ever have one of those thoughts that you think is

staying internal, but then you suddenly realize you've said it out loud? Such as ...

"Is *everything* here designed to kill you?"

Dad gives me a nudge in the ribs, trying to shut me up. So I elaborate.

"I'm just sayin' ... between angry bulls and fried butter, the odds of walking away intact aren't good."

Dad hangs his head in defeat, as I press the clown, "Do you get hazard pay?"

The clown narrows his brow, either offended at the notion, or baffled that he never thought to lobby for more money.

"Hey! Who wants a pop?" Dad quickly tries to change the subject, handing me some cash.

Sadly, he's using the local terminology for soda, and not giving me permission to slug the clown.

"Thanks," the clown says, "but I'm all good. Had three Red Bulls, in case I need to run real fast ... *from the bull*. Get it?"

The clown laughs at the irony, as I turn to Dad.

"You should give him your card."

"Stop," Dad grouses.

"It's only a matter of time."

"*GO*," Dad orders.

"Jeez ... 'stop, go' ... make up your mind," I jabber, as Linus and I walk to the concessions stand.

"Your dad seems a little stressed out," Linus observes. "Is he always like that?"

"Sort of, but I'm probably not helping," I confide. "All things considered, this is pretty animated for him. He hasn't been very engaged these last few months."

And just like that, it crosses my mind—Dad is starting to come out of his shell a bit. I hadn't readily noticed 'til now, with the maddening situation we're in. But he is a bit more aware these days. Since Linus is more of a genius than I'll ever be, I seek a second opinion.

"You'd think having a grim job like gravedigging would make you just check out and go through the motions," I surmise. "But he kind of seems like he's ... I don't know, more 'present' than he's been in a long time. Does that sound crazy?"

"Not at all," Linus says.

"Not even a little bit?"

Linus gives me a knowing look.

"I would guess it's a job that few people would be willing to do," he notes. "So the fact that your dad not only does it, but does it well—that means something. And lets him feel like he's making a contribution."

"But it's not like he ever *planned* to do it," I point out. "He just took it 'cuz he needed the work."

Linus gives me a smug smile—the kind of art form that only higher-functioning humans can master without getting smacked. So annoying.

"Or maybe the work needed him," he suggests.

Now, I get it that the brains of most teenagers are like revolving doors. Stuff goes in, and barely pauses for a dizzying glance before it whirls on out. But Linus seems to have taken a different approach—one where thoughts go in through a real door, and even take a seat in the lobby. In other words, he seems to truly process things, which is more than I can say for my diluted attention span, even on a good day.

"So you feel like our professions pick us, and not the other way around?" I wonder.

"Why not?" Linus presumes. "We're all born to do something."

I contemplate this angle in all its glory, which is part of the problem.

"But what about strippers?" I float. "Think about it—just because a woman has a big rack and no inhibitions, does that mean it's her only employment option?"

Now I've done it. Linus has gone into a trance. Apparently, some thoughts not only enter, but put up their feet and stay a while. I snap my fingers, forcing him to re-engage in the world.

"Oh, sorry," he mutters. "You said to think about strippers. So I did."

Genius or not, this proves that the mere mention of boobs will dumb any guy down. Happily, Linus pivots back to logic in no time.

"I usually request extra ice, especially on hot days," Linus crows, as we wait for sodas. "Depending on the temperature and the rate of melting, this can promote a higher ratio of overall liquid, which is more cost effective and more hydrating. But since it's evening, and the lines for ladies' rooms tend to be disproportionately longer than those for men, you may want to keep it status quo."

Wow, a silver tongue like that must make Linus a real snake charmer on dates. Hopefully, that's not what he thinks this is. I mean—as far as human beings go—Linus is okay, but he's nowhere near my type. I'm still pining for Rocky Tellerado, who remains the cover art for the trashy novel in my head.

And just then, I see him. No, not Rocky. Please, if that happened, I'd be so ridiculously tweaked I wouldn't even be speaking English, let alone finishing a sentence.

No, this vision is short and not so sweet, as in, *he's* back—my pint-sized pseudo stalker from Walmart, loitering by the hat stand. It has to be him, since there couldn't be that many stubby guys in parkas lurking in the shadows, even in this loony bin of a town.

I gasp and grab Linus's broomstick of an arm. "Who's that guy over there?"

"Which guy?"

"The mini Eskimo in the parka," I point.

"He's an Eskimo? I can't even see his face," Linus strains to get a look.

"I don't know for sure he's an Eskimo. But why else would somebody wear a flabby parka like that?"

"Ummm ... because he's cold?" Linus deduces, trying not to be too blatantly condescending.

"No, he's trying not to be seen, because he's following me," I insist. "He was at Walmart today."

"So were we," Linus blows it off.

"Yeah, but as weird as you are, even you weren't ducking on and off the tampon aisle."

Linus stares at me for a few seconds.

"Am I weird?"

If someone has to ask this question, then they were either born weird, or have embraced the small-town insanity a little too feverishly to notice their own demise. I try to let him down gently.

"Compared to the real world? Marginally. Compared to the rest of this town? Not so much."

Linus mulls it over, deciding if there's a compliment to be had anywhere in the vicinity. Then he gamely nods, "I'll take that."

I glance over to notice that "Tiny Bubbles" has floated off.

"He's gone. Where'd he go?"

"Maybe he went back in to watch the rodeo," Linus figures. "That's why everybody's here, you know."

Oh, so that's it? I thought everybody was here because there's absolutely nothing else to do in this town.

"You don't think it's even remotely possible I'm being followed?" I challenge. "Considering what's in my backpack?"

"I think you're being paranoid. Besides, if he were a hit man or something, he would have popped you by now. He wouldn't be browsing at hat stands."

Evidently, that venture is reserved for those who prefer horsing around, as Linus spots a prime sale item. "Speaking of which ..."

He points to a "mini" version of a cowboy hat, presumably designed for pets or dolls—giving both groups every right to revolt and kill their owners as a thank you.

Linus immediately whips out some cash, announcing, "You need this, as a souvenir from your first rodeo!"

Did he seriously just go there? If Linus doesn't consider this a date, then he must think it qualifies as a social event worth remembering. To say that I'm still on the fence about that one would imply that I've approached such an improbable fence and willingly climbed aboard. Yeah, no. But leave it to Linus, who is so thoroughly enthused there's no stopping him, and anyone who's ever witnessed the unnerving passion of a comic book convention knows that you don't stand between a geek and his toys.

Like a skinny, beardless Santa Clause, Linus proudly hands me one itty-bitty cowboy hat. As much as I know I will never find a single use for this decorative headwear, I don't have the heart to burst his square bubble.

"Um, thanks," I say.

Alas, here I am, literally with hat in hand, silently pleading for this day to end as we head back toward the arena. Unfortunately, Linus gets a squiggly hair of creativity up his butt and resolves that even if I'm not getting popped by a hit man, the evening should still go out with a bang … and party hats. For *very petite people.*

"Hey, you know who that'd be perfect for??" he giddily lights up, pointing to my backpack.

"Tell me you're kidding."

"Why not?" Linus persists. "This might be *his* first rodeo, too!"

While that may be true, my better judgment tells me it's gotta be patently inappropriate to dress up an urn like Mr. Potato Head. Even if that doesn't reserve you a spot in hell, surely it's enough to get you onto the waiting list. But Linus does make a valid argument, since we can't really know what William's hobbies were in life. Maybe he would be enjoying this evening, if he were here. In theory, he *is* here, in a portable sense. And with this being one of his last real social events above ground, is it totally crass to treat it as a celebration?

Besides, we're teenagers. And we're bored. Good luck

to anything that gets in our way.

I open my backpack and take out the urn. Linus carefully props the cowboy hat atop the lid, then takes aim with his camera.

"Wait! I have an idea!" Linus exclaims, channeling his inner Spielberg. "We need to make it look like he's a cowboy!"

Before I can decipher any crooked stream of logic, Linus grabs my arm, ushering us to the edge of the arena.

"Now hold it down at this angle," Linus points.

His enthusiasm is a little frightening, so I go along mostly to keep the hysteria in check ... and because the last thing I want is for Dad to notice what we're doing, since he wouldn't see the fun.

"All right, hurry up, will ya?" I grumble.

"Down a little more," Linus prods. "I'm trying to make it look like he's riding the bull."

Oh great—Linus feels the need to nitpick while I'm hanging over a railing. This whole thing is so uncomfortable, and reminds me that I should try to stretch more often. Now some commotion starts building at the other end of the arena. Who knows what's going on, since I can't crane my neck to look. I'm just trying to keep ahold of the urn while Linus checks focus.

"This is awesome!" Linus shrieks. "Hold it right there! One ... two ..."

Possibly it's the thrill of knowing that I'm doing something I shouldn't be doing, that my pulse starts racing. The noise builds to a frenzy, almost like the crowd is cheering me on. The whole scene moves at a dizzying pace, until all at once ...

Time stops, creating a deafening vacuum in my head.

Have you ever done something so blatantly wrong that you feel like you're watching it unfold in slow motion? Apparently, I'm hearing it in slo-mo, too, since Linus's voice sounds like my grandma's old answering machine when the batteries were low.

"Thhhhhhhrrreeeeeeeeee …"

The moment is so surreal, I feel like my head is spinning. Like I'm starting to lose my grip on reality. Or is it my grip on … *the urn??*

CLICK! The camera snaps just as an evil cackle rushes up behind me and whisks the urn out of my hands. Yes, you heard me. A psychotic clown has now burned me TWICE in the same day. I dare you to match that.

It turns out the commotion was the bull, chasing the clown, who—like most low-functioning minds—tends to gravitate toward the first shiny object it sees. Regrettably, that would be the urn, which was unluckily within reach as I was hanging over the railing, posing for what was bound to be a second-rate picture and is now undeniably one of the poorer decisions I've made in life.

Like I said, it's all happening so fast, it's pretty much a blur. All I know is, the clown is running through the arena *with the urn!!* A bull is chasing him and doesn't look like it's giving up anytime soon. In a move of desperation, I leap over the railing in hot pursuit, trying to retrieve poor William from this maniac before he becomes part of the arena dust. So now I'm chasing the bull that is chasing the clown who is juggling the urn.

I don't know if it's a case of massive guilt or ill-advised valor, but Linus has gotten in on the act, too, trying to distract the bull with his red T-shirt. My secret hope of Dad being in the bathroom and missing this spectacle is shattered when I look back and see that he's joined the mix, and is bringing up the rear.

Yes, it's that deranged.

The crowd goes wild, thinking it's all part of the paid entertainment: me trying to grab the urn, Linus playing matador, the clown running in circles, and Dad trying to keep me alive. The spectators love it. The authorities, however, aren't as charmed.

I don't want to bore you with legal stuff, but it seems there are a few, shall we say, "technicalities" about everything that happened. Disrupting the peace. Endangerment. Trespassing. Urinating in public (for the record, that was the clown). By the way, it appears he's a returning guest in the halls of justice, since the cops all know him on a first-name basis: "Leonard."

Uh huh. "Leonard the Clown."

Sure, he mentioned his name to Dad back when he rammed the van, since they had to exchange paperwork and all. But out of sheer annoyance, I didn't bother to process that this birdbrain has an alter ego outside of the face paint and silly shoes. Indeed, he does, and rumor has it Leonard is a bit wobbly when straddling the bounds of the law. I'd blame the silly shoes—except, in looking at him, there are endless things to blame. I wouldn't know where to begin.

The good news is everyone survived. Even William. Yes, I realize that's an unusual play on words, but the bottom line is that the Ziploc bag is still intact, and the urn only has a few scratches. In this alternate world, that counts as survival. And the police—undoubtedly used to local idiocy of this nature—eventually released us with a warning, so no charges were technically filed. Although I can't speak for Leonard, who may be doing community service until he's as old as Father Time.

The bad news is I will be walking funny for the rest of my life, since my ass will certainly be chewed out by morning.

You know that sinking feeling when you're waiting outside the principal's office because you've been busted doing something you know you shouldn't have been doing in the first place? You envision every possible punishment that could be awaiting you, which just makes it more excruciating. You inwardly run through all of the potential excuses you could use, discreetly trying to rehearse and figuring out tricks to conjure up tears in a moment's notice. Mainly, you just want to get your story straight, since school districts don't let you automatically call a lawyer. If I were more socially conscious, I would petition to change that. But since my motivation tends to come and go in waves, my best hope is to try to get through high school under the radar, and then date a law student in college—in case I don't grow out of this irresponsible phase anytime soon.

When facing parents who are visibly pissed, it really is like being summoned by the principal, since your fate is in their hands. Will you get off with just a warning, or will they throw the book at you? Sometimes it's best if they just lose it immediately, then at least you know where they stand.

But when they make you wait—either because they're silently figuring out your penance, or they can't even find the words to begin—that's the worst, since the hang time can be open-ended. I'm a busy person, you know. Can we get on with this?

Dad is pulling the silent treatment, and I can't tell what it means. He's been fuming ever since we got back to the motel, and it's making me bonkers. I debate whether I should be the first to inevitably bring up the touchy subject of the rodeo. Just rip off the Band-Aid and get it over with. But another part of my brain is telling me to keep quiet and hopefully this will all go away. For the record, that's also the part of my brain that teases me with the notion that I could actually be invisible. Tonight we found out how well that theory works, since the entire arena saw what happened. Then it dawns on me . . .

There was another participant in this ordeal. No, not Linus, or even that sad excuse of a clown. It was William, the "unwilling" participant who never got a say in the matter. I look over at his urn, now faintly scratched and covered in dust, and begin to process that I feel worse for him than I do for me. After all, William never banked on any of this attention. He just wanted a ride. He didn't ask to be abducted by a frizzy-haired psycho and become collateral damage in a high-speed chase with livestock. I doubt that any of these little escapades were envisioned when drawing up his prepaid plan. But here he is, all dinged and dirty, because of me.

I can't stand to see him like this. Whoever he was,

William deserves better. Dad may not be talking at the moment, but his words keep playing in my head ("This man deserves our respect").

Since nothing is happening yet on the yelling front, I figure it's probably still safe to make a dash to the bathroom. I retrieve a hand towel and start wiping the dust from the urn. I try to buff out the scratches, with minimal results. But the effort alone makes me feel a little better. It's not enough to make amends. But for the moment, it's something I can do to offer my apologies to this man I didn't know, but into whose life I've been determined to interfere and whose very existence I've seen fit to make a joke of. Right now, I don't need an exasperated parent asking, "What the hell is wrong with you?" I'm asking myself.

Dad watches me in silence, then comes over and takes the towel. He, too, starts to clean the urn. After a while, a few words do manage to find my throat.

"I'm sorry. I shouldn't have done that. To either of you."

I don't know what Dad's reaction is—I can't bring myself to look at him. I don't want to see the disappointment in his eyes, or anger in his face. I know this is bad. What I did, it's bad. It was wrong. And since I can't take back that moment, all I can do is hope that this moment will mercifully end. Which it does, when Dad leans down and kisses my forehead. One of those comforting, unexpected gestures that says, "I still love you, even though you're a colossal screw-up." He could scream at me. He *should* scream at me. But he doesn't. He chooses to show love, and the possibility of forgiveness.

Whatever I expected him to do, I assure you this wasn't it. I don't even want to imagine what Mom would have done. She's been known to have her "softy" moments, too, but I'd suspect that tonight's debacle is a scenario for which there is no working model for punishment. That's why I feel the need to punish myself for being so tragically inane. Which is why I can't hold back on what's been bugging me.

"Why do you think he had a stranger do this?"

"What?" Dad asks.

"William," I answer. "Why do you think he hired someone to take him home? Instead of having a family member or a friend do it?"

"I don't know. That was his choice."

"But would it be your choice?" I pose. "Wouldn't you want Mom, or me or Liv to take you home? And not somebody you never met?"

Dad considers this prospect, seemingly having an answer in his head, but defers, "Maybe he didn't have a family."

As much as that could be a possibility, I can't shake the image of the picture, wondering aloud, "But what about the baby?"

Dad lowers his brow, realizing that I've probably done a few other things I shouldn't have done, and in my moment of sentimental weakness, I've accidentally copped to it.

"What baby?" he pointedly raises.

It quickly becomes apparent that Dad's compassionate mood is starting to fade. Time is of the essence, so I weigh my options of whether to dodge the question or just confess my other unsanctioned activities. That is, until Dad beats me to the punch.

"You looked in that shoebox, didn't you?" he construes. "Even after I expressly told you not to?"

"Um ... I may have peeked a little."

"When??"

"Um ... when you were napping," I shrink.

Dad huffs, trying to hold it together, while I make excuses to the court.

"It was just sitting there," I weakly defend. "Under the bed, wrapped in your jacket, tied together with dental floss. Good call, by the way. That stuff is deceptively strong."

I was hoping Dad would laugh at that one. He doesn't. He just stares at me, trying not to come unglued.

"Why did you disobey me?" he sternly asks.

Judging from his tone, this is one of those moments where a cute, pithy response will only make things worse. Lying won't help, either, since nothing would sound logical. So I reach for the only possible escape hatch to get me out of this: the truth.

"Because I wanted to know what was so important that somebody would bury it with them."

Dad processes this stance for a minute, before reiterating, "I've told you, Greer. It's not our place to pry into this man's life. We have to honor his privacy."

Okay, sure—that sounds rational on the surface. It sounds respectful. So why can't I accept it and just stay out of William's business? That would be the humane thing to do. But I can't, because something else is bothering me now.

"But, if he had no family," I speculate, "what if we're the last people who care enough to look? Doesn't that honor him, as well?"

Okay, sure—that sounds a little irrational on the surface. It sounds like an excuse to be nosey. But I do mean it, and the whole thing seriously is bugging me. Dad regards my words, and something in his brain must have connected with what I said. He retrieves the box from under the bed and sourly eyes the tattered dental floss strapping that I hopelessly tried to rebuild.

"Really?" he lobs me a tired glance.

Guess I should purge "discreet rewrapping" from my life skills list.

Dad walks over with the shoebox. He gently removes the lid and takes a long look at the photograph of the baby in the striped blanket. His lips curl up into a warm smile. "I remember when you were that size. You had pink baby booties and a little yellow bib with an elephant on it."

"Oh yeah," I say. "I remember seeing them in my baby pictures."

"We still have them," Dad remarks. "Packed with some other things."

It hadn't occurred to me that my parents kept that stuff. Judging from the look on Dad's face, it was never a question that they would.

He lifts up the small box, focusing on the words: Bee and Live. Dad squints, perplexed.

"I know," I chime in, "I don't get it, either."

Dad fondly laughs to himself.

"I made something like this in wood shop, in junior

high," he recalls. "Only it was bigger, for my Grandpa's cigars."

Funny ... I never actually thought about my parents having their own childhood. I've only known them as adults, so to think that they were once my age is a foreign concept. Yes, I realize it's highly selfish and arrogant of me to assume that everything in their prior lives pales compared to the moment I was born—although, Liv would naturally expect that *her* birth was the real seminal moment for all involved. But it is curious, to picture what Mom and Dad were like when they were young, and whether they imagined that this is what their lives would be. Then I begin to wonder ...

What did William imagine for his life? Did everything happen how he thought it would? And out of everything in his life, what is it about the items in this shoebox that they hold so much significance? Especially the one remaining gem yet to be admired: the wooden foot.

"It's called a '*last*,'" Dad explains. "It's used by shoemakers. They craft the material for the shoe around the last, to make it a certain size."

"So it's not a wooden foot?"

"Well, it's a 'form' of a foot," Dad says. "Why? Did you think it was used for something else?"

"I don't know," I conclude. "Maybe he had a wooden leg, and he needed a wooden foot? Or maybe he was a department store window dresser who used mannequins made of wood, and there was a horrible termite infestation and this was all that was left."

"Or maybe he made shoes," Dad talks me down.

"That, too," I suppose.

Dad thoughtfully regards the box for a moment, before closing it again. He gives me a long look, acknowledging, "It's nice that you care. But it's important that you be respectful—to me, and Mr. Parkner. So no more going behind my back."

He takes my hand and gives it a squeeze, adding, "And no more running with the bulls. I'm too old for this."

I nod in agreement, as Dad puts the box away. All in all, things went better than expected. My ass is still intact, I'm not yet grounded for the rest of my natural life, and I even got a compliment. Not bad for a major screw-up with low expectations.

Kiss my wooden foot, Ginormous.

12

LAST DANCE

DAY THREE: Wednesday.
"Sprinkles Day."

"It's like a used car lot full of clunkers."

In the spirit of full disclosure, the above sentence was my grandma describing the dating pool at her assisted living home. But her words can prove handy for almost any scene of abundant mediocrity. And after all the hoopla surrounding "Sprinkles Day," the spectacle is beyond disappointing. A half-eaten cake donut, the crumbs of some sugary twist thing, and part of a glazed puck that looks like a puny spaceship that crashed into some sticky alien matter. Framing this sad masterpiece are a few loose sprinkles, dotting a flimsy trail along the desolate landscape of the box.

To be fair, I'm two hours late, since it's 8:00 a.m. and the feeding frenzy officially started at six. But it's not like the motel is crawling with customers (unlike other creatures), so one can do the math that Walter inhaled most of the box on his own. I'd demand my money back if I had legitimately paid for anything. Even so, I'm inclined to make a stink just on principle, on behalf of everyone who's ever felt royally screwed by a madly overhyped promotion. But before I can lodge a complaint, Walter gets a jump on me. For as lazy as he is, he's surprisingly quick in the race to humiliation.

"Looks like you folks caused quite a ruckus at the rodeo."

Walter holds up a newspaper, which—much to my horror—has a picture of the melee, under the headline "Out-of-Towners Cause Ruckus at Rodeo." Yes, we are front-page news on the road to nowhere ... and "ruckus" is a favorite noun 'round these parts.

"You're a little young to be carryin' a dead guy around," he wheezes.

I barely uphold a troubled stare. "Is there an appropriate age to *start?*"

Walter sniffs, as if holding some internal, deranged knowledge that he's playing close to his man-boobs. He's literally the dark underbelly of this town, since he has more than enough belly to spare. Luckily, Dad enters the lobby before any crackpot wisdom can be imparted. That is, until Walter's pudgy finger taps the newspaper.

"You know, technically, you had three people in the room," he sneers. "Normally, I'd charge extra for that."

Even from somebody who's clearly insane, that's some pretty flawed logic. It's not like we needed a rollaway bed or anything, and William only required one hand towel to dust off. All in all, he's a pretty low-maintenance guest.

Dad's face falls when he sees the paper, his mind probably running through all the avenues by which word of this little outing could make it back to Digby. Not to mention the chance that William's loved ones—whoever they are—could find this little blurb in cyberspace, and be none too pleased. If this were a big city, nobody would give a crap about some bumbling conga line chasing an urn. But here in Dullville, it's a banner headline and photo-op, and might even surpass the electric car fiasco as local folklore. If William wanted to go out with a bang, he's certainly doing it. If Dad wanted his job to go up in flames, this could be one avenue.

But I can't imagine that's what Dad had planned, and now I would be responsible if he did lose his job, since my idiotic little maneuver is what kicked off the conga line in the first place. In a feeble attempt to change the subject, my eyes fall upon the only thing that looks sadder than Dad's posture.

"It gets worse," I say, pointing to the donut box.

Perhaps that's not the best choice of words, since it's morning and the day has already gone to pot. But it underscores the reality that there are worse things than having our picture in the local newspaper. We could have ended up in mug shots, which we were thankfully able to dodge since the cops only "detained" us while they questioned witnesses. That's a bonus, since most universities tend to frown on incarceration, and it would shatter Mom's mission in life if I had a prison record instead of college transcripts.

Or suppose we were advertised on wanted posters, with a bounty on our heads. Walter would be speed dialing his gang of crazies, while trying to gag us with those nasty donuts, which could lead to a whole host of problems and bodily functions I can't even begin to cover here.

So when you consider how much more extreme things could be, we're still skating by on thin ice. Not wanting to dampen our good fortune—seeing as Walter is glaring at us with all the twitchiness of a bug zapper—Dad agrees it's time to make a fast getaway. From the motel, at least.

Off we go, in search of semi-real food and sanity ...

Which doesn't appear to be on the menu today, since all heads turn when we enter the diner. And why wouldn't they? The newspaper stand by the front door is empty, as this is apparently the only place on Earth that doesn't get their news from the internet. So there we are, at almost every table, splashed across the front page, ruckus and all.

Supposedly, everybody gets fifteen minutes of fame, which—on the surface—sounds exciting. The problem is, we don't get to decide *when* it happens, or for *what*. We prepare for it, but only for the *fun* versions of fame: playing air guitar, singing into our hairbrush, practicing our acceptance speech in front of the bathroom mirror. Don't be a hater—you know you've done it.

But if this is my one and only shot at celebrity, then notoriety thoroughly blows. I'm standing in front of an angry pack of media hounds, who cling to their utensils like pitchforks, itching to start the public flogging after their tenth coffee refill. The hazardous combination of caffeine and flatware has disaster written all over it. I swear some kid in the corner looks like he's wadding up sugar packets into stones. Just brand a scarlet "L" on my forehead already, to give them a clear target and get it over with. Yep, to say that fame is wildly overrated would be a massive understatement.

And then there's the problem of my so-called

bodyguard, who has ducked outside to answer his cell. Are you kidding me? Now? Who could it be that's important enough for Dad to abandon his baby in this moment of turmoil? Maybe Digby caught the news of us trotting through a dustbowl with an angry bovine. Or maybe Mom got a snippy text alert from the GPS on my phone, telling her that we had veered off the main road and driven into madness. Or maybe it's God, who felt it was time for an intervention. Pick one.

"Two and a half?" the snippy hostess stews, still bitter about the lack of reward money on the horizon, especially now that the whole town is well aware of our infamy and is gunning for us.

A more mature person might let this comment slide by without reprisal. But aside from the fact that maturity's never really been my thing, now I'm pissed off. How dare she say that about William? Yeah, yeah, I know—I said it first. But that was yesterday, and one rodeo ago. I've seen too much now. I have frantically run for my life and have emerged to tell the tale. Don't even try to mess with me, chick.

"Three," I lean in, with menacing scorn. "No booster chair."

And that, my friends, is how it's done. This little hostess cupcake is quaking in her cheap boots as she leads us to our table. I use the word "us" as in William and me. Dad's still outside, talking to whoever.

We take a seat. Or rather, I do, and set William on the table. Everyone in the restaurant is all gaga about the urn, like it's some shiny, glittery toy. I made that mistake at first, too. But now I know better. For whatever reason,

William expected unknown people to haul him and his shoebox to his final destination. And he probably figured that at least one of us would feel entitled enough to snoop through his personal belongings. So he wanted to keep us guessing. Why else would anyone carry around a wooden foot? William knew the drill—life is short, so make it interesting and damn the ridicule. I say he should hold his lid high and forget snubs like the one coming from the next table.

"You folks got some real screwed up ideas," a slimy-looking man snarls.

Obviously, the voice of experience there.

"Can it, Hank," Lola commands, as she arrives with the coffeepot.

Lola is nowhere near as tall as Ginormous, but just now, she had a bit of a beastly streak. I'm fairly awestruck. Between her and William, I'm starting to learn that mighty things come in small packages. Or rather, mighty *unexpected* things.

"Coffee?" she asks.

"Sure."

Lola pours me a cup, and then it happens ... the inescapable moment of uncertainty. The pause as we both stare at the urn. With the whole restaurant watching, we silently debate if this is the moment to make it real. The moment to prove that William *is* one of us. Growing a pair, we dare to go for it. I push William's empty coffee cup toward Lola, who happily obliges and fills it.

Hank snorts something obnoxious at the next table.

"Shut your pie hole," Lola growls, smacking his arm as she walks away.

That's fabulous. Who knew we'd find a personal henchman in the form of a slightly squatty waitress in orthopedic shoes? And since Hank's one of those patrons who's permanently "out to lunch," it doesn't hurt to have a buffer.

Dad's still outside on his call, leaving William and me to face our cranky audience. It's like a room full of Pesters, watching our every move. My former self would likely have seen this as a moment of retreat. But the new me is uniquely liberated, not caring anymore what people think. They're gonna stare, no matter what. So why bother wasting more energy on the inevitable?

Even though this is a novel approach for me, I have no illusions that my higher mind is bursting with a new form of clarity. It's more like the Steaming Buddha somehow crawled into my skull while I slept—which, theoretically, would make my head explode, due to the space constraints. But like a jolly band of squatters, his directives keep finding shadowy corners to hide in, while they whisper into the dark recesses of my brain.

"*Everyone in this life is your brother.*" Sorry, but I've met way too many annoying people to embrace that much extended family.

"*Do not encourage angry confrontations.*" Well, if these people would just lose the newspapers and surf the web like everyone else, it wouldn't be such an issue, would it?

But the words that keep coming back aren't about driving, since after all, the whole "driving lesson" angle is more of a footnote to any one-on-one Buddha time. The only things you really remember with him are the moments of random oddities, masquerading as enlightenment. Such as his remark about my dad's job, that he *"gives people the last material gift they get on this earth."*

I mull the whole thing over. What gifts have *I* given William, other than a hard time, repeated embarrassment and legal trouble? Granted, I haven't exactly been warm and fuzzy in my approach. I've carted him around in my backpack, only because of parental intimidation. I've also taken him out of said backpack, but mostly to make fun of him with party hats, or to impose my own form of public retribution upon Dad. Perhaps it's time to turn the tide, and steer this annoying little detour in a more positive direction.

Which brings us to this moment … where the whole restaurant is watching, as William sits with a cup of coffee in front of him. If ever there were a chance to live out loud, it's here and now. Except …

I'm at a loss as to what to do. "Petting" the urn is highly inappropriate, since he's not a puppy. Ventriloquism—although potentially hilarious—seems rather tacky. Cradling the urn is beyond awkward on too many levels. So I do what most people do over coffee: make conversation.

"How do you take it?" I extend the sugar bowl.

Maybe it's the hardware, but William strikes me as a straight-up kind of guy. No cream or sugar here.

"My grandma used to tell me that coffee stunts your growth. Is that true?"

As the words leave my mouth, it occurs to me that I'm talking to someone now a fraction of their former size, packed into a traveling container. *Awk-ward.*

Dad comes back, before I step in it any further.

"That was the mechanic," he says, taking a seat. "The van's going to be ready this afternoon."

"Really???" I beam.

"Really, and then we can be on the road."

"Sweet!" I cheerily raise a toast to William's coffee cup.

Dad casts me a disapproving frown. "Did you learn nothing last night?"

"Now, wait," I begin. "In my own defense, just let me explain." Glancing around the restaurant, I point out, "These people look at William—"

"Mr. Parkner—"

I toss him a slanted eye. "In the last twenty-four hours, we've been stranded, run for our lives, been arrested, made the front page, and a clown publicly pissed himself over this whole thing. Not to mention we're now facing a potential lynch mob with small utensils. I think we can all be on a first-name basis at this point."

I doubt that Dad sees my logic, but he's just too wiped to argue.

"Go on," he sighs, drained.

"These people look at William like he's some kind of spooky prop that gives them the 'willies.' Kind of ironic, really."

Dad just lobs me a tired look. Got it ... funny ain't selling. Move along.

"But we know that he was a person, who had a life. And in that life, he likely ate breakfast and had coffee. So, instead of hiding him away, why not include him? And treat him like the person he was? Even if we have to ... *guess* on the details?"

Dad ponders this approach, before noticing that everyone in the restaurant is staring at us. Any hopes of flying under the radar for our remaining time in purgatory quickly dissolve before our eyes. The old version of Dad would have shut down, bypassing breakfast just to avoid a scene. But one cagey glance at Hank, who squirms at the next table, and Dad decides it's time to grab the bull by the balls, yet again. Miraculously, his rational, uptight side gives in to his impudent, "What you lookin' at?" side. I always assumed that side existed—since we all have one—but never saw clear evidence of it until now.

Dad opens a menu and plops it down in front of William's coffee cup. As Lola returns with her scratchpad, Dad loudly announces, "Our guest will have the giant scramble. Extra bacon." He clutches a butter knife and glowers at Hank. "'Cuz that's how we roll."

Hank flinches, uncomfortable.

Wow. So that happened. Honestly, the only thing preventing a mic drop right now is the fact that Dad doesn't have a mic.

Lola whispers, "So, um … do you want me to bring him food for real? Or are we still doing this for show?"

Since Dad's not used to being covert, he hasn't thought that far ahead.

"Why don't you split with William?" I suggest. "He's a light eater."

The intrigue of being in on a secret plan whips Lola's giggle meter into a frenzy. "I'll bring y'all an extra fork," she winks.

Being young with a decent metabolism, I order French toast with berries and whip cream, to enjoy life while I still can. Dad gives me an amused grin as Lola walks away.

"What?" I ask, puzzled.

Dad laughs to himself. "Nothing."

Maybe it's the relief of almost being out of this town—or just the sheer satisfaction of sticking it to the local busybodies—but for the first time on this entire trip, Dad actually looks like he's enjoying himself.

"I should call your mom and give her an update," he says.

"You gonna tell her we got arrested?"

"We were only 'detained,'" he reminds, in a hushed tone.

"Oh, that'll help. Mom's big on semantics."

You know whenever parents are determined to keep secrets from one another, even when they won't cop to it, because they typically try to pass it off as polite concern.

"I'd ... prefer to ... not ... worry her, right now," Dad stammers.

That's the trick—keep it hazy and noncommittal. Then when you chicken out, you're not officially a liar.

"I'll shut up if you do," I offer.

"Deal."

We shake on our sly little pact. Dad catches sight of a grumpy Hank, who chews his pancakes like cud. Dad realizes it's probably best to not advertise our schedule in front of a disgruntled throng, so he ticks his head toward the front door.

"I'm gonna ... go *outside* to call."

I look to the urn, vowing, "No worries. We got this."

Dad steps away as I lock a bitchy glare onto Hank.

This yahoo has no clue what he's gotten himself into, considering that stare-downs have always been my thing. Even Liv—who loves stare-downs more than life—has never been able to match me, and eventually cracks under duress. Good luck, weasel. It's on.

Hank breaks a slow sweat, feeling the pressure mounting, as he starts to choke on his pancakes. I don't technically know the Heimlich maneuver, so if that blueberry goes down the wrong pipe … oh well.

My steely gaze makes Hank gag even harder, until Charlene strolls by, giving him a walloping smack on the back. Apparently, everybody hates this jerk. She may have saved his pathetic weenie life, but I'd bet she mostly just felt like hitting him. I can't blame her. I've only been stuck here since yesterday and I'm ready to go ballistic. But her and Lola *live* here. If they're only at smacking level, then they're practically as serene as the Buddha.

*

"Don't let the door hit you on the way out."

That's what Grandma regularly said about any relatives or other company who overstayed their welcome. Although she didn't say it to their faces, she let loose once the door had closed and their backsides were moving along their merry path. It's like she just had to get it out, or burst.

I know the feeling.

I could almost hear those words banging around in Walter's thick head, but I wasn't about to give him the satisfaction of spewing them first. Just the thought of getting out of this town made me pack my stuff so fast, that door wouldn't come close to leaving a mark. Sure, if I'd had the chance to unscrew the hinges, I would have gleefully flung the lumber back toward Sir Sloth, along with a few lasting insults. But unlike Walter, time was wearing thin, so he had only my impatience to thank for his survival. Even Dad was itching to get out of that dump before that madman could hold us for ransom for the whole "third person in the room" caveat. So we paid the bill and hoofed it, in case Walter's lunatic fringe was planning to surround the place.

To say he's blown our return business is being generous. I'd rather sleep in a gorilla's armpit.

The only door in danger of hitting me now is the van door, which I flung open to throw our stuff inside. Dad's finishing whatever paperwork he has to do with the mechanics, and then—if miracles do exist—we're outta here. I'm just trying to shove everything in so we can scram as soon as possible. Even William gets strapped into his own seat, in case we two-wheel around any corners as we peel off into the sunset. After all this, we don't need to tempt Murphy's Law and spill the passenger.

I'm so ready to leave. For the love of God, what is up with these guys? The mechanics keep yapping at Dad, explaining this and pointing out that, and blah, blah, blah. It's as if they're still trying to wipe away the stink of the electric car fiasco by proving they're somewhat legitimate at their jobs. If they don't shut up soon, I swear I'll highjack a tire from the lobby and start rolling down the highway.

The only thing that stops me from launching into a full-on hissy fit is the ringing of my phone.

"Liv?"

A long silence, until she responds, "I'm in my car."

Perfect. The one time my desperate pleas effectively hit a nerve with her, the guilt kicks in too late.

"Oh, it's all good," I convey. "You don't have to come get me. We're getting out of here today! That is, if these mechanics ever shut their traps."

The muffled sounds on the other end of the line, however, make it clear that she's not sharing my joy. Liv's never been a crier, so I'm not even sure that I'm hearing what I think I'm hearing.

"What's going on?" I ask.

"I don't know if I can do it," she softly says.

There are times in life when you raise a question because you genuinely want to know the answer ... and then there are times when you don't really want to know the answer, but you know you have to ask. This is one of those times. The second one.

"Do what?"

Liv relates that, yes, she's in her car. But, no, she's not driving. She's in a parking lot, outside of a clinic. A women's clinic, where women go for many reasons. Some want to get pregnant, some don't. And some who are pregnant arrive in their cars, and walk through the front doors. Once they get inside, then some continue on through the next door, while others turn around and walk back out the front door ... without going through the second door. Instead, they return to their car, and wonder if it's time to drive away. Some look back. Some don't.

And some pick up their cell phones, because they just need to hear another voice ... or the silence of someone listening on the other end.

So far, silence is winning out, since I'm not coming up with many words. My mind races, debating, "Does she want to be talked *out* of it? Or talked *into* it?" Regardless of the circumstance, Liv has always been someone who knows her own mind, even if that mind can be pretty cluttered. But now, it seems like she's asking for advice— without overtly asking. Maybe the act of picking up the phone is her way of asking. So I feel like I should, at least, try to say *something*.

"Are you all right?"

Another long silence. But I hear her breathing, so she hasn't completely thrown in the towel on this discussion. I applaud her commitment, since I would have checked out on me long before now.

"I don't know," she confides. "I thought I could handle it. Just walk in and get it over with. But ... once I got in there, I just ... I just wanted to come back out here. Is that crazy?"

"No. You have to go with what you feel."

"But that's just it," Liv contends. "I don't know what I feel."

Neither do I. This is such a major life decision, I don't even know how to make sense of it, let alone be remotely helpful. But maybe some things aren't meant to make sense. They just need to ... *happen*. And what comes after those moments is what helps us make sense of everything, even if we're not aware that's what we're doing. The answers start somewhere, which inspires me to say what we both know has to be said.

"Maybe it's time you talk to Mom."

I halfway expect Liv to immediately shoot down this suggestion. But the silence kicks in again, so she must, at least, be thinking about it. I mean, she had to know it was inevitable for Mom and Dad to find out, and that one day, the whole thing would become real—not just in her body, but in her mind, too. Stepping into that clinic, and seeing the faces of the women in the waiting room, and seeing the forms she had to fill out, and hearing the nurse call her name before she could walk through that second door—that made it real. The only chance of turning back would be the turning toward the front door, and getting back into her car. And those steps, too, are real.

Liv deeply sighs, "She's gonna lose it."

I thought the same thing last night, with Dad. Trust me, there have been plenty of borderline moments when it was warranted, but if ever he had a reason to lose his mind at me, the ruckus at the rodeo was definitely it. But he held it together. He didn't even rip me the new one I thought he would. He was mad, of course. Wouldn't you be? But he was also understanding, and forgiving, and loving. He was a parent. And even when we really, *really* screw up ... that's who they are. And I guess that's why we get so scared when we do something wrong. Not because they won't love us ... but because they'll love us in spite of us. And the enormity of that idea, that anybody could love us *that much,* is pretty huge.

"She's not gonna lose it." As soon as I say the words, I concede, "Okay, she might lose it a little bit. But she loves you. She can help you figure this out."

"But how am I supposed to tell her?" Liv implores. "And see the disappointment in her face? Because you know it'll be there. You know it will."

"But she can't help you if you don't tell her," I caution. "Then you're in this totally alone."

Even though she hasn't said it out loud, we both know that last part is true, since Liv's loser boyfriend has never been one to step up to the plate and could hardly be labeled a rational adult. And it goes without saying that I'm a pretty meager support system. If there's any hope of dealing with this, it will have to be with Mom—especially since Dad is only now starting to peek out of his shell, and we don't want to scare him like a hermit crab. Besides, this kind of thing is more Mom's territory, anyway.

"Look at the bright side," I urge. "She's been managing a half-cocked Bridezilla all week, so there's not much that scares her at this point."

That elicits a faint laugh from Liv.

"When are you coming back?" she asks.

"Hopefully by the weekend. As long as we avoid clowns."

The mechanics finally release their verbal stranglehold on Dad, so Liv and I wrap it up. Right now, it's enough for her to handle one parent. My job is to keep the other one intact until we get home.

As Dad walks toward the van, I glance at the urn, and wonder if William was a parent. There was that picture of the baby amongst his things. Is there a child out there who ever called just to hear the sound of his voice? And what did his voice sound like? I'll never know, because all

I know about William is what's strapped into the back seat. And before you go off on a tangent, I already tried exploring the internet to see if he had a Facebook page, or Instagram, or something. He didn't, at least not that I could find. Which is kind of maddening, because it would be so much easier if he just splashed his life out there.

But maybe that's the argument to be made: it was *his* life. So if William chose to fly under the radar, busybodies like me will have to work around it. Hey, we have it easy compared to the old days. Grandma used to talk about things called "socials," where people would get together and mingle, since they didn't have computers back then. Sometimes they didn't even have phones, which is beyond primitive. Whatever the case, back in her time, people had to make a real effort to get to know each other. Not like today, where it's a few clicks and you can have entire relationships where you never even meet.

We get so used to everyone oversharing online, that when people don't offer up their info, we forget where else to look. It's almost like we lose sight of the person who's actually there, right in front of us. Until, one day, they're gone; and then it's too late. Which is why I speak up, as Dad gets into the van.

"I have to make a quick stop," I instruct.

He looks at me in shock. Considering that all I've been doing for two days is bitching about how much I want to get out of here, he probably thinks this is a joke. Yesterday, it would have been. But today—much to my chagrin— there is one surprising thing in this town that deserves a few extra minutes of my time.

"I want to say goodbye to Linus."

Dad starts to smirk, so I immediately shut him down.

"Don't get all happy. He's *so* not my type. It's just …
he did jump in front of a bull for me. You did, too.
Thanks for that, by the way."

Dad nods, letting me ramble.

"But Linus had no legal obligation to save me," I add.
"So I feel like, after everything, it'd be pretty cold to just
up and leave."

"You're right," Dad agrees. "So where are we going?"

That's the thing—after last night's upping of his social
clout, I fully expected Linus to be holding court at his
favorite booth at Walmart. After all, how often does the
local bookworm get to brag about a brush with the law?
But when I texted him, he returned some cryptic message
about meeting at a street corner. In the big city, this
generally means someone is either a drug dealer, a hooker,
or homeless. Or a combination of each. But here, it could
mean anything, so we just go with the flow, straight to the
corner of "Thingy Bob" and "Somethin' Something."

When we arrive, Linus looks more nervous than usual.
I didn't mention anything about us leaving, so I doubt
he's planning to propose in a last-ditch effort to get out
of this town. But he is sweating a little. What if he really is
a drug dealer, and we're about to walk into a shakedown?
Aww, frick! If I end up getting arrested again because of
Linus's poor planning, I swear I'm gonna snap his skinny
little neck.

"What's up with you?" I grill him. "You seem
squirrely. Even more than usual."

"I'm fine," Linus skirts the issue.

I pull William's urn out of my backpack, figuring

there's strength in numbers.

"So listen, um ... I know you two got kind of attached, so we just wanted to come by because—"

"Hang on," Linus checks his watch. "There's something I've gotta do first."

"Uh, well ... we're kinda pressed for time," I stress.

Linus appears unfazed by my dilemma.

"Yeah, but if I don't do this now, I may never have the guts to go through with it again," he touts. "And it's something I have to do!"

"What could you possibly have to do that could be more important than me getting out of here?" I hound.

"Wait—you're leaving already?" Linus's face falls.

Before I can answer, he checks his watch again, then suddenly bolts into the middle of the street, dodging a couple of cars.

"Where's he going?" Dad halts.

"I don't know," I huff. "Maybe to rob the bank? So whacked. If he's that tapped out, I would have loaned him my nine dollars."

But quick cash is not on the agenda, as Linus stops in the intersection, and stands there. Not moving.

"What's he doing?" Dad rails, exasperated. "Trying to get himself killed?"

Then it hits both of us: what if Linus *is* trying to get himself killed? Why else would somebody stand in the middle of the street if they weren't trying to end it all?

"Stay here!" Dad commands, as he dashes toward the intersection. Oh, geez. How am I ever gonna explain this one to Mom if things go radically wrong? Not that they haven't already, considering that Dad nearly got gored by a bull trying to save my moronic ass. I barely weaseled out of that one. But now he's running between cars to save a dork in traffic, all because I had to be a thoughtful person and go out of my way to bid farewell. I can't win.

Dad tries to grab Linus. "C'mon!"

"No, I have to do this!"

"It's not worth it!" Dad shouts.

"Yes, it is! I've never done anything to make an audacious statement to the world! I have to change that!"

"This isn't the way to do it!" Dad pleads.

"This is my only chance!" Linus affirms. "It's now or never!"

I can't say if it's guilt, stupidity or blind panic, but something about seeing these guys in the throws of traffic makes me run into the street after them. Plus, it's one more excuse to chew out Linus, who could not be more annoying at the moment.

"Linus! Get a grip!" I order. "I don't have time for hysterics!"

Dad gapes at me in horror.

"What are you doing out here??"

"Trying to slap some sense into him!" I fire back, eyeballing Linus. "And I *will* slap you, if you don't stop this!"

"Go ahead! Slap me, then!" Linus dares.

Hmmm ... that was a bit unexpected. But in this case, I'm all for it. I look to Dad, who shrugs and ticks his head toward the accused, which—we all know—is a parent's mode of giving permission, without verbalizing it. So I slap Linus. Not incredibly hard, but hard enough to make me feel better. He doesn't budge.

"Happy now?" Linus pompously throws down the gauntlet.

Damn. Who knew Linus had the balls to endure female intimidation? Unless—and I'm truly creeping myself out here—that was the objective all along? *Ewwww.*

Cars begin honking, protesting our blockade of their route to mind-numbing oblivion.

"What's your problem?" I interrogate Linus.

"You can't stop me from doing this!" he asserts. "I'm going through with it!"

"Why??" I hold up William's urn. "So you can end up like William? Trust me, he's been through a lot these last few days, and he could tell you, death's a hassle!"

"I don't want to die!" Linus shrieks.

"Then why are you in the street??" Dad and I holler together.

And then, the strains of the mad plan come together … as in, strains of music. Playing from a boom box, manned by some pimply-faced guy on the sidewalk. Not just any music—dance music. As in, *disco* dance music. You know, that whole "esoteric movement" thing Linus holds in such high esteem? That disco.

And then … Linus begins to move. Not toward the sidewalk. Not toward safety. No. That would make life too easy. Instead, he moves his hips and his feet. As in, disco dancing.

And then … others join in. From out of nowhere, people start rushing into the street. Dancing to the disco music, in one mass, somewhat coordinated herd. You get the picture, right?

"*A FLASH MOB??*" I screech. "That's what this is all about?"

Dad cringes at the people swirling about him.

"What's happening?" he recoils.

Linus gleefully dances, fully in his glory.

"It's my first one!" he beams.

Oh hell no, I'm not letting him off that easily.

"Seriously, Linus, you people have to catch up to the times! I did my first flash mob two years ago!"

"*You did??*" Dad flinches.

"*I did??*" I echo, horrified that I needlessly spilled a secret.

As usual, Linus is still focused on being an insufferable manager.

"If you're gonna stay out here, you guys have to dance!" he demands.

Great ... now Linus expects us to somehow keep those steps in time with their disco-Pagan hybrid.

"I don't dance!" Dad objects.

"Doesn't the music move you?" Linus bellows.

The look on Dad's face suggests that a bowel movement is more likely.

"This is a nightmare," Dad groans.

"You're only NOW realizing that??" I chastise him.

"Hey!" Linus barks. "Kick up your feet, party people!"

While the strains of disco music thump all around us, my first instinct is to clobber someone with the nearest blunt object. But since that would be the urn— and probably involve an assault charge—I restrain myself. Then, like an expanding rash, the repetitive rhythm takes hold, and my legs start to twitch. Don't tell anyone, but despite my best intentions to be a hater, I'm sort of digging this whole disco throwback. Maybe it's the disarmingly catchy beat with vapid lyrics. Or maybe being notorious for a night has now made me want to blend in, for safety's sake. Or maybe I just want Linus to shut up, so I'm willing to play along. For whatever inexplicable reason, I start dancing, too.

"It's not that hard!" I reassure Dad, as I follow the steps.

He stares at me, bewildered, then snatches William from my hands.

"I'm not dancing!" Dad howls, attempting to stomp off.

Well, *that's* a tad bitchy, and not even realistic. You ever try making a beeline through a crowd? Not so easy, is it? Now try doing it when the crowd is shaking their groove thing all over the place. Uh huh. Did he learn nothing from the rodeo debacle? There is no "stunt urn." He's juggling the real deal. And whether spillage is covered in Digby's malpractice insurance is anyone's guess. That's when the real dancing begins in Dad's head, with images of lawsuits and clients wafting in the breeze.

Dad soon realizes he has no choice but to join this disco inferno, if there's any hope of getting out of this mess intact. So he starts to move with the music—against his will, of course, and highly uncoordinated. I could be more generous, bestowing an "'A' for effort," but let's not get carried away. He's about a "C+" on a good day. But at least he's moving. And then—brace yourself …

He starts to enjoy it.

With my track record, you probably assume I'm being

my usual cynical self here. Believe me, it's enticing. But I swear I'm not making this up. He's genuinely having fun. Or that's how it looks. Dad's even smiling. And pretty soon, he's laughing. And even when he's able to get to a spot in the crowd where he could potentially worm his way to the curb without turning all parties into roadkill, he doesn't take advantage of the out. He keeps dancing, with William.

For all I know, this could be the first time he's dared to show his moves in public. I don't know if I've ever seen him dance, except for in my baby videos when I wasn't such a harsh critic. But it's probably safe to say this is the last time William will dance in this life. Because even though he's in an urn, it's still him. And he's moving, because Dad is holding him up as he tries to go through the motions and not be too much of an embarrassment. Which means everyone can see the shiny urn above the crowd. Everyone, including ...

My stalker. Or perhaps it's now "*our* stalker," with his parka and stout little legs trying to weave through the crowd toward Dad and the urn. I suddenly comprehend that this shifty Eskimo isn't after me—he's after William. I don't know what range of shady business our departed friend was into in life, but it's obvious that this wee henchman is not gonna "fuh-gettaboutit" anytime soon.

But what's up with the mafia that they send a guy barely bigger than a Cannoli to do the job? Surely this isn't the best they could do. Aside from not being tall enough to bash a head, this munchkin looks incapable of even handling a kneecap or two. On top of that, he's bouncing off the town crazies like it's a mosh pit, and can't get anywhere close to Dad and William. Talk about shortsightedness from upper management.

"Isn't this fun???" Linus joyfully shouts over the music.

Normally, I'd try to shoot down such tiresome exuberance. But it's obvious that Linus's disco fever has been burning for a while, and no aversion to polyester or platforms is gonna temper that calling. In fact, as much as he may have wanted to seize the moment, it's more like it seized him—and that's a joy you don't find every day. So I let him bask in his giddiness, with no snarky retort, since the whole thing is strangely amusing ... even if we are being followed.

Which doesn't appear to be the case anymore. I turn towards Dad and don't see any sign of the disco duck, who must have waddled back to his swamp. No parkas or menacing Eskimos to be found. Not that I'm searching that hard, because all I can grasp right now is the expression on Dad's face. It's something I haven't seen in a *lonnnnnggg* time. A look that is unmistakable, and impossible to fake. A look of pure, unabashed joy.

I stop dancing and just stare at him, wanting to take in every second of this sight, which is beyond wild. After all, Dad's dancing with an urn. How many times am I gonna see that?

And if Dad's face is any indication, they're both having the time of their life.

13

LAST EXIT

DAY FOUR (Part One): Thursday.

"We're being followed by a midget Eskimo."

Dad lowers his brow. "What?"

"You heard me. This whole thing stinks worse than that bull."

I know the chances of Dad believing my diatribe are slim, but in the interest of full disclosure, I think I should mention to him that a peewee goon is on our tail. I had originally thought that once we left the funny farms, all would be right with the world again. But even though we're back on the road, I still can't shake the feeling that we haven't seen the last of our batty little friend. To humor me, Dad checks the rearview mirror.

"There's no one following us," he calmly says.

"You sure? He's pretty teeny."

I look back and see a speck in the distance.

"That could be him. That puny dot. He could be spying on us with, like, high-powered telescope glasses."

Dad sighs, obviously not amused.

"Dad, I'm not kidding! He's a psycho midget Eskimo!

I saw him, like, three times!"

"All right, calm down," Dad insists. "First of all, the appropriate term is 'little person.'"

"Oh come on! We're gonna do this now?? Our lives are in danger and you want to be politically correct?"

"Indulge me, like I indulge you," Dad implores. "And if you want to get technical, was he a midget? Or a dwarf?"

"There's a difference?"

"Yes. Were his limbs proportional?"

"I don't know," I admit. "I couldn't tell, with his parka."

"He wore a parka?"

"He wears it all the time."

"Ah," Dad catches on. "Which is why he must be an Eskimo, right?"

"Ex-*actly.*"

"Uh huh. Greer, you need to lay off the conspiracy theories. I know they've been a source of amusement for you throughout this trip, but we're almost there, and this'll all be over soon. So just relax."

"But Dad—" I protest.

"*Enough.*"

I fold my arms and slump down in the passenger seat, doing my best pout. Dad's seen my routine enough times to know that this whole exercise is going nowhere, but it has to run its course, and pretty soon I'll be rambling about something else. As much as it irks me that he has my number, there is something oddly comforting in the realization that he knows me well enough to leave well enough alone. Unlike others, who are determined to push my buttons—like Linus did yesterday, when all the dancing was over, and it came time to say goodbye.

"I thought you might stay a little longer," Linus bemoaned.

"Why would I do that?"

"I don't know ... maybe because you had fun here?"

No, you didn't hear that wrong. He really said that, before he noticed the horrified look on my face. Linus did his best to salvage the moment, even though it was more of a lost cause than Leonard the Clown.

"You seemed to be enjoying yourself just now, when you were dancing."

"Yeah, 'cuz I knew we're leaving," I carped. "Why wouldn't I dance?"

Linus looked down, dejected, which only emphasized what a crass and heartless bitch I was being.

Admittedly, sometimes my tendency to speak my mind has a way of highlighting my equally keen lack of tact. It's a vicious circle, which had accidentally swallowed Linus. Time to cough him up.

"Look, I just don't fit in here," I tried to explain.

"But I do," Linus said quietly.

That's when I clued in that my rationale was precisely that ... *mine*. Which means it didn't necessarily apply to anyone else. It's not like Linus gets a choice about where he lives. Sure, he could run away, but where would he go? Either the cult police or the real police would find him sooner or later. So he makes the best of it, which is an approach I should probably try more often.

"I'm sure there are worse places to be stranded," Linus posited.

"I keep trying to convince myself of that," I said.

"I just wish you didn't have to leave so soon," Linus moped.

"I know, but we gotta get William to Michigan. It's contractual."

"Does he have family there?"

"Beats me," I shrugged. "I mean, if he had family, wouldn't they be driving him? It'd be the civilized thing to do."

Linus fretted with genuine concern. "What if he's alone? What if he's buried in obscurity?"

Those words keep ringing in my head, as we drive. A few days ago, all I cared about was getting back home. But it's starting to sink in that everybody has their own version of home. For Linus, it's a dusty little pit stop in the heart of humdrum. And even though I find it a disturbing freak show, he's perfectly content—sitting at his booth in Walmart, buying dinky cowboy hats, and getting delirious with disco fever. Now that I think about it, Linus is one of the happiest people I've seen in a long time. And he even tried to be something of a friend to me, when all I did was bash him for being an outcast. Truth is, *I* was the outcast. And Linus helped me get through those two insanely long days, by making me feel like I was welcomed, even in a place I didn't want to be.

And what about William? He has a home. Or, *had* a home. I mean, we picked him up in Boulder, but maybe Michigan was his real home. Or where he grew up. And if that's the case …

"*Where's his friggin' family??*" I blurt out.

"What?" Dad asks, as he drives.

"William's family! You know, the people who are supposed to love him? Who are supposed to take care of him? How come they're not doing this, and taking him home to be buried? Or put on a mantle, or whatever he wanted? Huh?"

"Greer, we've discussed this," Dad calmly answers.

"And it doesn't make any sense, does it?"

"I've told you—"

"I know, I know, it's none of our business!" I dismiss. "But whose business is it? The funeral home's? Is that all William is to them? A sale for their business?"

"What's gotten into you?" Dad presses, taken aback.

Apparently, it's a pretty wacky mix. Start with Linus's words, throw in a dash of the Buddha (which is more like a heaping tablespoon, let's be honest), and stir in a whole other mess of things I've never bothered to contemplate before. And, then, to top it off, sprinkle with a dusting of William.

Take it easy. I can practically hear the self-righteous wheels cranking in your head, griping, "When are the powder jokes gonna end? Just give it a rest already." No, *you* give it a rest. C'mon, now—on this entire trip, if ever there was an appropriate time for a dusting analogy, this has got to be it. And I'll even go one further, and say that William would agree. Yeah, you heard right. William would appreciate my thought process, because he gets me. He understands the sarcasm of teenagers, because even if he didn't have kids of his own, he was a kid, himself, at one time. And when you think about it, that's the only real experience any parent has when going into the job, so why not put it to good use?

Maybe that's why Grandma's advice was generally a little nuts. Not because she was getting senile or forgetful—but because she *remembered*. She remembered what it was like to be young and dopey and uninformed. So no matter what she said, she knew it would come off as flakey. "You stop bleeding." "It's all gibberish." The whole point of her advice was that she wanted me to recall her words, even if I couldn't decode them at the time. She knew that one day, they would all make sense in their own way. Even what she said about people like Linus sometimes being "book smart and life stupid." At first, it would seem she missed the mark on that one, since—despite his quirks—Linus isn't a total loon. Then I remember the other half of her analogy:

"But at least they know the facts."

Yes. Linus knows the facts, enough to point them out to me. He said I owe it to William to know his story, since I'm sharing his final days. Not to mention, our final days together. So in that sense ... I owe it to me, too.

Which is why I feel I have full license to be nosey. Since Dad keeps insisting we have to stay out of the details of William's life, questions will get me nowhere. But I can't let go of the idea that, for some unknown reason, he wanted strangers to do this. To drive his remains across multiple states, to deliver him to a funeral home, to do whatever he had planned for his big sendoff. Maybe he wanted strangers because he was hoping they'd keep their distance. That's Dad's hypothesis, anyway. Stand aside and no one gets hurt.

But what if the hurt started long before this? Long before anyone picked up his urn and put it into a van?

What if the hurt was the reason for planning everything ahead of time? Because there was no one else to do the job? Don't get me wrong—as a rule, I'd be all too happy to just look the other way and let someone else find the answers. Between puberty, Ginormous expectations, and the quest for a driver's license, I've got enough on my plate.

But even with what little I know about William—which is next to nothing—I do know that I want to see him treated right. That he can't just be thrown into a hole and forgotten. What if Linus hit it on the head, and William is alone, and is gonna be buried in obscurity? He doesn't deserve that. Nobody does. And once we deliver him to the funeral home, that's my last chance to do something about it. So I've got to think fast …

Which isn't going too well, since I still have no plan after we finally arrive in Michigan.

While Dad and the funeral home guy are off gabbing about some technical mishmash, I take a look at the paperwork that came in William's box, and see the "next of kin" listing: his mother, and her address. Even though I've never been to this city before, I don't have time for the tour. So I scribble the information in the manic scrawl of someone who knows they're about to do something pretty radical, and is so pumped from adrenaline, they can't help but write ninety miles an hour. Then I redo it, because I totally can't read what I just wrote.

Truthfully, I don't have much of a plan, other than to go and stare down that lame excuse of a mother who had the audacity to abandon her son in his hour of need and leave his welfare to others. And even if she turns out to be some hideous, angry, spitting and spewing boil on the face of humanity, I'll at least give her a dirty look before running for my life.

Seriously, how could she do that to William? Was he an awful son? Or was she just an awful mother? There's only one way to find out, because sometimes you just gotta say "Piss on the consequences," and do what you believe is right. No matter how crazy it may be on the surface.

Because, sometimes … you have to stick your neck out for a friend.

If only I had paid more attention in Geography, then I could figure out where I'm going with a compass and stick. Or I might recognize what a homing pigeon looks like, and bribe their services for a day. Does a homing pigeon look different than a regular pigeon? You'd think I'd have radar for such creatures, considering that all I've wanted to do for days is go home. But now that I have to find someone else's home, who knows if the pigeon theory would hold up, so this whole train of thought could be completely bogus and I might just be talking out of my butt. As you've certainly noticed, it wouldn't be the first time.

The desk clerk at the funeral home gave me directions, and I left a note for Dad, just so he knows I wasn't abducted. And in case this sorry excuse for a mother turns out to be some mean old witch who tries to make stew out of visitors, it never hurts to leave a paper trail.

In this case, it's more like a trail of fumes, since I can only afford the bus—which doesn't lend itself to making a quick exit, if this woman's a total whack job. But since money and sanity don't grow on trees, I'm taking the cheap route toward disaster in a getaway vehicle that resembles a sloth on wheels. Frick, could this driver go any slower? I saw that old movie *Speed*. I know buses can go at least fifty-five miles per hour, so something approaching the speed limit would be nice. Besides, the more time I have to mull over my ill-conceived plan, the more likely that I'll back out. And I can't do that, even when my phone rings and it's Dad. I look at the display, debating whether to answer, until it eventually goes to voice mail. I know he must be losing his mind, so I text him, *"No biggie. Am fine. Call u soon."* I feel bad for blowing him off, but I've got to do this for William, wherever it takes me …

Which ends up being the porch of a remodeled Victorian home, that now serves as a nursing care center. Suddenly, this vague strategy is looking even more doomed, basically pounding it into me that I should take a breath before going off the deep end next time. Oh sure, strong-arming old ladies for a good cause sounds noble, until it dawns on you that they're *old ladies*. Kinda tough to cast that as a positive.

I keep having visions of my grandma, since she was in one of these places. How would I have felt if some smart-ass kid showed up to berate her over something that was none of their business? That some meddlesome brat felt justified in venting about presumed wrongs, when they didn't even know the whole story? If someone tried to do that to my grandma, it would royally tick me off. So why wouldn't William be pissed if I did that to his mom? What if he gets so bent out of shape he chooses to relentlessly haunt me, with eerie groaning and clanging chains? Or slowly drive me mad by constantly moving my stuff around? It could happen, since he already has plenty of reasons to hate me from the afterlife. I'd say the bungled rodeo was the tip of that iceberg.

Clearly, I just need to stop being so pathetically full of myself and be grateful that fate has been pretty forgiving to this point, and hasn't punished my idiocy too severely ... yet. It's one thing to push the boundaries with William himself, but to break those boundaries and start dragging his family into my half-baked theories—that's going too far. So I should leave.

But I'm not. My feet aren't moving. Because it hits me —what if it's not going too far? What if I haven't gone far enough yet? What if William *wanted* me to come here and find out whatever it is I'm supposed to find out? I know it sounds like a reach, but think about it: nothing about this trip has been normal, or—let's face it—congenial, so why expect those things now, when we're in the home stretch? Maybe now is the time to pull out all the stops, because when am I ever gonna get this chance again? And who's gonna speak up for William, if I don't?

"Hello?"

Whoa! I really wish the universe would stop butting in.

"Were you looking for someone?"

Crap, I've been made. An attendant is poking her head out the front door, since squatters on the porch tend to draw attention.

"Um, I think so," I reply. "William Parkner's mother?"

"Oh, you mean Mrs. Bridges? His stepmother?"

Stepmother? I was in such a frenzy to scour the paperwork, I must have glossed over that little detail.

"I guess so," I concede. "This was the address."

"Come on in," the attendant offers. "I'll show you to her room."

Walking down the hallway, I try to keep an eye peeled for escape routes, in case this stepmother turns out to be the fairy-tale version: mean, scary, and not in the mood for cute, young girls. Even though those stories usually end with singing birds and happy songs, some pretty gnarly stuff happens along the way. And frankly, my patience is pretty tapped out at the moment, so it's best to just keep things moving and bag the cheery music.

As we arrive at the room, the attendant lightly knocks on the open door.

"Helen?"

An African-American woman turns around. "Yes?"

"There's a visitor here," the attendant says.

Whatever I thought was going to happen, I wasn't prepared for this. Not only has the attendant left, leaving me face-to-face with William's stepmother, but the woman I'm looking at is not hideous, and she's not even that old ... maybe early forties. I'm so confused.

"Can I help you?" she asks.

"Uh," I stammer. "Mrs. Bridges?"

"That's my mom," the woman answers, stepping aside to reveal her elderly mother, who lies in bed, asleep.

I feel like I've skipped a few breaths by now, looking at the fragile image of a sweet-faced, aging woman, dozing softly in her bed. Every scenario I ever made up about the mother who couldn't bother to pick up her son instantly goes out the window.

"You're William's family? William Parkner?"

"You mean Billy," she says.

"I mean *William*," I stress, a tad defensive.

"Only his teachers called him that," she clarifies. "Well, and his mom, whenever he was in trouble. Which, come to think of it, happened a fair amount. So yes, he was William, but most of the time he was Billy."

She warmly extends her hand, "My name's Helen. Billy's stepsister."

I shake her hand, offering, "I'm Greer, reluctantly. William's ... *delivery attendant*."

Helen looks at me, puzzled, until I clarify, "My dad and I brought him here from Boulder."

A gleam of recognition flashes across her face. "So you're the one."

Oh no, she's heard something. This can't be good. It had to be the rodeo debacle, in all its front-page glory. Otherwise, how could she possibly know the depths of my stubris? And then, the short answer emerges, as in ...

The midget Eskimo. Yeah, *him*. The same guy whose been chasing me and whose little head now pops into the room like a zit. He and I both shriek upon seeing each other, since I'm as scary to him as he is to me.

"What's *she* doing here??" the midget Eskimo wails.

"What's *he* doing here??" I snarl.

"I thought I was finally getting a break from you!"

"What are you talking about?" I protest. "*You're* stalking *me!*"

"*Stalking?!?* I've been trying to save you from yourself and get Billy here intact, before you go spraying him like a snow blower!"

"Calm down, Cid," Helen interjects. "She got him here, didn't she?"

"Barely!" he sneers.

"And by the way, how does she even recognize you?" Helen pointedly grills him. "You were supposed to blend in, remember?"

Cid throws up his hands in disgust.

"*Hello!* Do you know what a tall order that is?"

You gotta admit—when people say funny stuff without realizing it's funny, the whole thing is all the more hilarious. Which is why I can't help snickering. Even Helen can't contain a small laugh. Cid, however, doesn't see the humor.

"Oh that's nice," he growls. "Laugh at the dwarf's expense!"

"So you're a dwarf?" I innocently ask.

"What did you think I was?"

Some answers are better left unsaid. But I justify it by at least telling the truth, no matter how tacky.

"A midget Eskimo," I mumble.

Cid just stares at me, so I try to dig out.

"With the parka and all ... from a distance ..."

Cid tosses Helen a tired look. "Do you see what I've had to put up with?"

"Relax, Cid," Helen advises. "The poor girl thought she was being stalked."

"Yeah, I thought you were a hit man," I echo.

"*Bodyguard,*" a pissy Cid insists.

Seriously, this guy's gotta stop, 'cause I can only hold back snide laughter for so long. Helen sees that I'm about to lose it, so she steps in to salvage things.

"Would you mind giving us a minute?" she coaxes our little friend.

"Oh sure, the room's getting crowded, so kick the *dwarf* out," Cid grumbles. "*That* helps."

He tromps off, as Helen shuts the door.

"You have to forgive Cid. He's a little touchy."

"Then he might want to rethink his wardrobe," I propose.

Helen assesses me, amused. "Okay, 'reluctantly Greer.' Let's get to it. What brings you here?"

"I ... looked at the paperwork that came with William's urn," I confess. "I'm sorry, I know it was none of my business. Dad kept telling me not to pry, but ..."

Helen reads my hesitation. "What?"

"I just couldn't stop wondering why no family came to pick him up."

"Ah," Helen catches on. "So you wanted to see what type of family would leave him behind."

I weakly nod, "Although, judging from everything here, I don't think that's what happened."

I look over at Helen's frail mother, sleeping soundly, and all I know is that it was *me* who was judging them; assuming that I knew the whole story, when it's obvious I knew nothing.

"Besides, it doesn't matter what I think. Dad was right. It's none of my business. I'm really sorry I bothered you."

Even though Helen looks at me with kindness, I simply can't bear it anymore. I'm such an idiot. So I hastily leave the room and charge down the hall, toward the front porch ... anywhere that I can breathe.

I flop down onto the front steps. My head is a wreck. I don't know if it's a panic attack, or just blatant embarrassment, but I just had to get out of there. What did I expect, barging into these people's lives, all full of myself? Helen has an old, weak mother who maybe can't even get out of bed, so how could she leave her for a road trip?

And Cid? Who knows what's going on there. Talk about having friends in low places. Not to mention, he's drastically tilted toward the angry scale. And who could fault William if he didn't want to experience that vibe on his bon voyage to the world? Keeping that little tornado on the fringe was a wise choice. So William ended up with me and Dad, which would have been somewhat civilized and respectful, if I had just listened to reason and not come here in the first place. But here I am, sitting on the steps of an old folks' home, realizing to my horror ...

I don't remember which bus I took. Now I have no clue how to get back to the funeral home. For all concerned, I suppose it's time to return one of Dad's bazillion phone calls. So I start dialing, until screeching tires come to a stop in front of the house. Dad jumps out of the van, charging toward me up the walk.

"*GREER!!* What are you doing??" he rages. "Just leaving like that?! I've been losing my mind!"

Even if I knew how to explain, I'm not sure I could find the words, since I've never been so thankful to see anyone. I know I'm in major trouble, and I absolutely deserve to be. But there's nothing I can say to make this whole thing sound any better.

"How dare you just *leave!*" he continues in a fit. "Do you have any idea what could have happened??"

I don't want to think about that—kids never do. But parents have to think about that stuff, because that's their job as parents. Which is certainly why he's so upset, and angry, and relieved, all at the same time. And me? Hey, I'm a total mess, too. So I do the only thing that feels natural, and leap up from the step and run into his arms.

Dad holds me tighter than he ever has. I can feel his hands shaking, and realize just how scared he was at the whole thought of me taking off. That's one of the reasons I'm crying—because I'm sorry that I worried him so much, and I'm sorry that I'm such a monumental screw up, and am so grateful to be back in a comforting place.

Not to mention, the whole bus issue has gone away, which is a welcome bonus, and all the more reason for tears of joy. But I'll keep that part to myself.

"I'm sorry, Dad," I softly say.

He lets out a giant sigh and holds me tighter.

"Don't ever do that to me again," he pleads. "You can't imagine how much you scared me. Don't EVER do that again! Promise me."

"I promise."

Dad releases his grip and scours my face for answers.

"Why did you leave? Huh? What are you doing here?"

The front door opens. Helen steps out onto the porch.

"Is she okay?" Helen asks.

Dad looks at both of us, confused. "What's going on?"

"You didn't tell your daddy where you were going?" Helen scolds me.

She folds her arms, with a "tsk tsk" sound and resting bitch face that comes out of nowhere. Damn, girl. I've been shut down before, but that is some true artistry.

"Greer?" Dad persists.

Just when I had started feeling better, my heart sinks again. All this time, Dad's been warning me to stay out of William's business. How do I tell him that I've done just the opposite and barged right into his family life?

As luck would have it, I don't have to. Cid's happy to do it for me.

"Oh great, your co-conspirator's joining in," Cid snarks, as he passes us on the walkway.

Dad stops cold at this peculiar little sight. He raises an eyebrow, mouthing, *"The midget Eskimo??"*

Fully aware that the guy is like a diminutive pit bull that can't let anything go, I wait until Cid is a comfortable distance on before I whisper, "He's technically a dwarf."

Dad discreetly watches Cid from a safe distance.

"I know," I elaborate. "With the parka and all, it's hard to tell."

Not only does Cid have the jaws of a dog, but apparently, he has the hearing of one, as well.

"Why are you people so friggin' fascinated with my wardrobe?!?" he seethes. "Don't you have *bigger* things to worry about?"

Here we go again with the unintentional humor. I'm trying to hold it in, but my throat's crackling, so snorting can't be far off. Helen covers her mouth, as her shoulders convulse, and even Dad's lip curls up in amusement. Along with a leash, Cid could use a better agent if he's gonna be playing such hostile rooms.

Helen pulls herself together, gesturing to Dad and me, "Maybe you should come inside."

Dad looks at me and pointedly questions, "Greer, why did you come here?"

Since running away is noticeably not my strong suit, I reach for the only answer that makes sense, even though I'll probably get into even more trouble for saying it.

"To meet William's family."

14

LAST WISHES

DAY FOUR (Part Two): Still Thursday.

I give up. I got us into this one. I could have left it alone. But, no. After being chased by a psycho clown, an angry bull, a dancing dork, and a dwarf Eskimo, I'm sitting in an old folks' home, getting the backstory of a guy in an urn. How's that for a week's work?

And since Cid is unable to keep his little trap shut, Helen's bound to know about the rodeo. So it's baffling how she could even think of inviting us into their lives.

Yet, here we are, getting to know more about William. And not through paperwork or peculiar keepsakes, but through people who actually knew him. Not just the portable version of him; but the genuine, full-sized, real-life *him*. It's one thing to have a vague concept of a person through a few details or mementos. But it's another thing entirely to hear stories of them, emphasizing not how they died, but how they lived. Helen talks of William's compassion, his humor and sense of adventure, along with one of his central beliefs: "Without endings, you don't have beginnings."

I'd never thought of it like that. On the surface, endings can seem like a harsh concept, since they bring the hammer down on stuff. But that's not always a bad thing, and can even be a relief, depending on what's happening. Take relationships ...

I've only dated a few times, but I know from plenty of bitching friends that not all relationships are good. Some are just hopeless. First, the griping starts, then the nitpicking, then the paranoia, and then the whole thing shrivels up faster than Liv's bank account after a shopping binge.

As if that isn't cheery enough, we've also got to accept that some endings are already a lock, regardless of what we do. Take childhood ...

As a kid, all we really know is what we're born into. Our family, our home, our neighborhood. It's our version of normal, until we get older, and things change on their own—namely our bodies. Once objects start growing in every possible direction, that's when all bets are off. By the age of twelve, I began to realize that nothing's permanent—even my Aunt Marilyn's perm, which inevitably grows out, no matter how many chemicals she dumps on it. So endings are part of the bargain, even when they're fried from a body wave.

From the sound of it, William had reconciled that his own time was ending.

"He'd known for a while, but didn't want to burden us, even though we never would have felt that way," Helen says. "So he made all of the arrangements."

William's cancer was found about a year ago. It was already fairly advanced, and had begun to spread. He did chemo and radiation for a while, but they took such a toll, he eventually made the decision to stop.

"Billy chose to spend his remaining time by living his life," Helen describes. "Truly *living*. He traveled, visited friends. Not emailed them, but made a point to meet up, face-to-face. He came home to visit a while back. We cooked, we laughed, we danced …"

Danced? I nudge Dad. At least we got that part right.

"He spent time with Mama," Helen continues. "Since he didn't get that luxury of time with his own mother."

Helen explains how William's mother died from a heart attack when he was sixteen. Wow. I'm only a few months away from being that old, and I can't imagine what it'd be like to lose either of my parents. Sure, there's times when they drive me bananas and I need a break from them. Isn't that the general rule with families? But we know we can hang out again when we're ready; that our time apart is just temporary.

"Is that how you became his stepsister?" I ask.

"Yes, in theory," Helen clarifies. "We were neighbors. He was best friends with my older brother, Barry. Billy and Barry. 'The King Bees' we used to call them. Which is why they were frequently in trouble. Neither of them thought the rules applied to them. So our mothers bonded … usually trying to control their sons."

"Where was William's dad?" I pose.

"Greer—" Dad whispers, cautioning me.

"It's okay," Helen grants. "Billy worshipped his dad, even though he never really knew him."

She tells us how his father was killed in Vietnam, when William was a baby. His dad only got to see him as a newborn, when he was home on leave. I figure that must be the picture we found in William's things—the one of the parents' hands, holding the baby. No wonder it meant so much to him.

"Our moms pulled each other through the dark times," Helen recalls. "Billy's mom was young and inexperienced, so my mom took her under her wing. She felt for her, since they were both raising kids alone."

Alone? It sounds like Helen didn't grow up with a father either, although I don't want to be intrusive. Dad's right about that. None of this is any of our business. But hey, I can't always control my face when it does this contorting thing, which invariably gives me away, so Helen obliges.

"My dad left when we were little," Helen imparts. "Went out for cigarettes one day and never came back. He wasn't much into the 'family' thing, so it didn't make a whole lot of difference after he was gone. Except there was a lot less shouting."

Since William already knew what it was like to not have a dad, he and Barry became inseparable.

"That was a time when some people still found it curious for black and white kids to be friends," Helen points out. "But it didn't matter to Billy, or our moms."

Helen recounts how their mothers had made a pact, that if anything happened to either of them, the other would be godmother to their kids. That's how William ended up living with Helen's family, to finish his last two years of high school.

"Our moms didn't want our lives disrupted any more than necessary."

Even though I know it's in poor taste to butt in, I can't take it anymore.

"Seeing as we're talkin' disruptions," I interject, "What's with the dwarf in the parka? He's a crabby little handful."

Dad buries his face, mortified.

"Oh, I know," Helen chuckles. "But Cid means well, even if his approach could use some ... *refinement.*"

"Or some sedatives," I suggest. "He should lose the winter gear, because that guy severely needs to chill."

Turns out, Cid was another neighbor when they were growing up. He was the weird kid who lived down the street. Every block has one. You know them: the kid who shows up at your doorstep for trick or treating—the *day after* Halloween. They've got no costume, since their inherent strangeness is scary enough, and then have the gall to employ the law of averages, figuring that you're bound to have leftover candy and know that you'll all too happily unload it just to get this creepy little brat off your porch. Uh huh. *That* kid.

To top it off, Cid was super small for his age, and when it became obvious he wasn't gonna grow beyond fun size, kids at school would constantly pick on him.

"One day, a group of kids at the playground were throwing rocks at Cid," Helen relays. "Billy went over and told them to stop. He even took a swing at one of the boys who wouldn't quit, and that nearly got him expelled."

From that moment on, Cid idolized William. That mini basket case had barely ever had anyone take an interest in him, let alone protect him. So Cid was committed to returning the favor, by making sure William's ashes arrived safely home. That's when we showed up, and, well … you know the rest.

"So that little maniac was trying to do a good thing?"

"*Greer!*" Dad admonishes.

"Sorry," I sigh, "But you gotta agree, his methods need some work."

Speaking of work, I'm curious about what William did for a living. Eventually, the conversation goes there.

"He was a paramedic," Helen answers. "After losing his parents, he decided he wanted to help people, and try to spare them that pain. And he did. He saved a lot of lives over the years."

Not that it's any of my business—not that any of this is—but in learning more about William, and how fabulous he sounds, it strikes me as odd that Helen hasn't mentioned him having a family of his own. He sounds like he'd be a pretty cool dad, not to mention a total catch. I'm not trying to be intrusive, but in case you're not too observant, I have a tendency to blurt things out.

"What about a wife and kids?"

Dad gives me a pained *"Are you serious?"* look. He's clearly tapped, and can't even dignify my meddling with a verbal response.

At least Helen hasn't tuned me out, which is frankly astonishing. Most people would have bailed hours ago.

"Billy was engaged, a long time ago," she relates. "His girlfriend from college. I'd never seen him that much in love. But she broke his heart a few months before the wedding. Said she was in love with someone else. It shattered Billy. After that, maybe it was intentional—or maybe just unconscious—but he never came close to marriage again. He had some girlfriends over the years, but he never made a commitment … until Delilah. The love of his life."

"Where is she now?" I impulsively ask.

"In one of those boxes you brought," Helen says matter-of-factly.

I slowly turn to Dad, who nervously gulps. I can't tell if it's the fear of "Holy crap, did I forget someone?" or "Holy crap, there were only two boxes, and one of them had a wooden foot."

"Well, um … there was a shoe box," Dad hesitates.

"About the size of Cid," I describe.

"And then, there was a *smaller* box," Dad stammers.

"About the size of Cid's shoe," I add.

Helen's not remotely fazed. "That's her."

Given that she's not having a breakdown over this detail, I'm hoping I'm wrong when I squirm, "Was William a serial killer or something?"

"Not unless he made a career choice he never mentioned," she laughs.

That sounds comforting, hypothetically, but even I catch on enough to point out the obvious.

"I'd say that's something you might not want to advertise."

Helen gives me a reassuring grin.

"Delilah was a sweet, gentle, loving little cat," she clarifies. "And Billy was never anything but gentle in return."

A cat? Huh. I kinda pictured William as a dog person.

"They were on a call one day, and as they were loading

the ambulance, he noticed this beautiful tuxedo cat in a tree. She had long, black fur with a white chest, white paws, and a white diamond on her forehead. She was gorgeous, and had him smitten in no time."

Helen tells us how Delilah and her brother Samson had been left behind when their previous owner passed away. After the woman died, her prick husband coldly turned out the animals when he moved. So other neighbors took turns feeding them.

"For months, Billy would go on his own time, before and after work, to check on her," Helen recalls. "His buddies would rib him about his 'sweetheart.' Here he was this strong, tough guy, who could handle anything. But he just melted around that little cat. He bonded with her like nothing else in his life. I think because he knew what it was like to feel abandoned ... and scared that you're not going to find your way home."

Several people had tried to bring the pair in, but Samson had pretty much turned into an outdoor cat, and Delilah wanted to be with her brother. He was her protector, and she would have been lost without him.

"And then one day, she was," Helen sighs. "Samson had a tendency to go into the street, and a car came whizzing by one night. You can guess the rest."

After Samson died, Delilah spiraled downward. She would disappear for days at a time, reemerging with a filthy coat, riddled with fleas.

"Who knows where she was hiding, but she was terrified."

William coaxed her into a carrier and took her to the vet. She was in pretty bad shape, and at first, they didn't even know if she was going to make it. But she did. And he finally got to bring her home.

"You could say they rescued each other," Helen offers. "He became the parent she thought she'd lost, and she became the child he didn't know he needed. She gave him a purpose beyond himself. His years with her were some of the happiest of his life. Even on his most grueling days, she was like a light in the darkness."

But not long after William was diagnosed, Delilah became sick, as well.

"It was almost like she tried to take away some of his burden," Helen describes. "Pretty soon, she started failing, too. She died a few weeks before him, and that's when it seemed like he started giving up. He had been holding on to care for her—being her lifeline, just like she was his. But once she was gone, I think he lost his will to live."

A long silence fills the room, until Dad speaks up.

"There wasn't anything that could be done to save him?"

I look at Dad, struck by the fact that he's interested in William's life. All this time, Dad's told me to not get involved. But now, even he looks a little sad, like he's—I don't know—*mourning* William in a way. Or maybe he's trying to make sense of how a man only a few years older than him is gone, and the random unfairness of it all.

I don't know what Helen does for a living, but whatever it is, she should add "mind reader" to her resume, because she really seems to understand people. So she manages to give Dad a sincere, but compassionate, answer.

"As much as he tried to save lives, Billy understood that at a certain point, you have to stop trying. Because the body knows when its life is leaving ... even if we're trying to convince it otherwise."

On the surface, that could sound sad. But like every surface, there is something underneath. I'm even starting to see that about Grandma's wonky theories and kooky advice. If we look beyond what's there, that's when we get to the point.

It's pretty amazing, really, how William spent his final months. Going beyond the surface, tying up the loose ends, and taking the steps he needed to find the point of it all. And by doing so ...

Maybe the last life he saved was his own.

I know what you're thinking. With all my snooping, I missed the obvious. The one question that has prevailed ever since I busted through the dental floss wrapping in the motel room; the question that would be too bizarre to voice in everyday life. But this is *my* life. Bizarre has pitched a tent and set up camp.

"What's up with the wooden foot?"

Oh, don't worry. I asked. And I gotta say, I'm a little bummed that the answer wasn't nearly as nutso as I had expected. But it was the answer that was the last missing piece of William's life, and that could be what's got me bummed. There's nothing left to ask.

"Billy's grandfather owned a shop where he fixed shoes," Helen clarified. "Shortly before Billy's dad went off to war, his father made wooden forms of his feet."

"They're called 'lasts,'" I added, not to be smug ... but because it's one of the few facts I've actually retained.

"That's right," Helen said. "Billy's grandfather promised to make his son the finest pair of dress shoes he'd ever own, to use when he came home."

Helen paused, thoughtfully.

"But Billy's dad never made it back. His helicopter was shot down. His remains were never found."

Even Dad choked up at that idea. Seeing grieving families firsthand, he understands how much they need that closure. And to think that William's family never got that opportunity, is very sad. That pain is real. I could see it on Dad's face. And for the first time, I valued the importance of his job, and the responsibility he takes on in doing it right.

"The 'lasts' became just that," Helen concluded. "The last pieces of Billy's dad."

I wasn't even sure if I should mention anything, but it's not like she's not gonna notice ...

"There was only one," I said, "With his stuff."

"I know," Helen said. "The other was buried with Billy's grandfather. He wanted to keep a piece of his son with him."

Then she added, almost unconsciously, "Good parents always want to keep their children close."

I don't know what was going through Dad's mind. He didn't say anything. Just reached over and clutched my hand and held it tight. And although I never realized it before, I was grateful for that luxury. A father's hand was something William hadn't felt since he was a baby.

Then I looked at Helen, holding her mom's hand, and it occurred to me that she'd lost a parent, too. Not her deadbeat dad who walked out years ago. But her mom, who raised her and her brother, and took in William—and who was now stuck in that bed, in some sort of mental limbo.

Her mom stirred as Helen comforted her.

"Ssshh ... it's all right, Mama."

Whatever is going on with her mom is obviously the reason that William didn't want Helen to leave, to bring him home. Which is why he arranged everything, and had strangers do the driving.

After hearing about his dad, even William's fear of flying made sense. As cornball as it seemed at first, now I get it. The important thing is that all of William's last wishes be honored. Which is why I was beyond shocked when Helen invited us to his funeral.

"Excuse me?"

"I think he'd want you there," Helen declared.

"Even after ... *everything??*"

That got a laugh out of Helen, who determined, "Billy would have liked it that you cared enough to come here. Because he probably would have done the same thing."

Realizing that I was being commended for prying—the one thing I'd been repeatedly told not to do—I was massively confused. So I turned to Dad, to see where his head would be with all this.

"Dad?"

After all the bonehead things that have happened, I kind of feel like I owe William the respect of attending his service. It'd be the decent thing to do, right? But then again, with all the bonehead things that have happened, pushing our luck may not be the brightest approach. So perhaps it's better to get out while we can. I don't think William would necessarily hold it against us. I mean, if he's not pissed enough to start haunting us by now, we may be in the clear.

Dad thought about it, for what felt like an eternity. Then he looked at me and smiled in a way that I hadn't seen in a long time. The smile that crosses your face when you look at something, or someone, and in that moment, you can't imagine looking anywhere else. It's the only place your eyes want to be.

"Okay," he said.

And it was. It was okay. Even when we ended up in another friggin' Walmart, buying me a dress and getting Dad a tie. It was okay, because it was for William. And when you do things purely from the heart, your actions come from a place that makes everything okay, even when they're ass-backwards.

Which brings me to this moment, as I sit outside our latest motel room (a definite improvement from the last hovel) and gaze into the night sky.

When it gets down to it, I'm not sure what I was expecting by confronting William's family. I have no idea what I would have done if things had turned out differently—if they weren't open to talking about him, or if they'd kicked me out. Sometimes, the terror of a conversation is not in what's being said, but the unknown of what might come out of it.

But just like today, people can surprise you. It does happen on occasion. And sometimes, we even surprise ourselves, with the places we're willing to go, what we're willing to fight for, and what we end up caring about.

"You told her?" I question Liv, who has just called.

"Yeah," she says.

"And?"

Liv starts to recount the conversation she had today with our other parental unit—confronting the unknown, by telling Mom that she's pregnant.

At first, there were no words coming out of Mom ... which is, like, *beyond* unfathomable. Liv said she just sat there, looking into the distance. Who knows if it was the past or the future she was seeing—all Liv could tell is that it was somewhere far away. After a while, Mom gave a glimpse into that place.

"Your father and I were in college," Mom began. "We'd only been dating a few months, so it was still fairly new. Even though we tried to be responsible, there were times when we weren't so careful. At one point, I was three weeks late on my period, and was losing my mind."

I can't even picture Mom being young and stupid. She was probably already a control freak by third grade, so it's stunning to think that she ever had a moment of being borderline irresponsible. Even though the pregnancy test was negative, she was still spazzed out enough to leave it in the wastebasket, where Grandma saw it. That's when things got interesting.

"Your grandma found me curled up on my bed, crying. The tears were a combination of relief and terror and confusion. I didn't know what to think. Your dad and I already knew we were in love. But part of me wondered what I would have done if that test had been positive.

Would that love have been enough to sustain us?"

"What did Grandma say?" Liv asked.

Apparently, Mom let out one of those sighs that only happen when exhausted resignation has surpassed any hope of logic. A perfect lead-in for Grandma's response: "Dandelions get a bad rap."

Classic. Mom sought life advice and Grandma talked lawn care.

"You know your grandma," Mom surrendered. "She had a way with words. But that time, I think she knew I needed actual advice."

Ordinarily, I'd inject something sarcastic about that prospect, since advice shouldn't have to come with a magnifying glass and decoder ring. All right, fine ... I am being sarcastic. But at long last, I dare say I've cracked the code to Grandma's bonker theories: look beyond the surface, and that's when you see the point.

It seems Mom had caught onto that angle, too.

Mom said Grandma talked about how people can look at dandelions as a nuisance; an intrusion that needs to be removed, because they mar the perfect landscape that we're trying to cultivate. Sometimes, they still pop up, no matter what you do to protect against them. But Grandma argued that dandelions don't get the credit they deserve, because they're resilient and bring color to their surroundings. So why should dandelions get blamed for just sprouting up? They're not the worst thing."

"Wow ... with the pregnancy test and all, you'd think she would have gone for a fertilizer angle," I surmise.

"*Right??*" Liv agrees.

'So then what happened?"

Liv tells how Mom just gave her a long look—which sounded eerily similar to the look that Dad gave me today. Must be some psychic married thing. Then Mom put her arms around Liv and held her. The type of hug that keeps you close, keeps you safe, but still gives you space to breathe. I know that hug—I got one today, too.

"We're going to get through this," Mom promised her. "Together."

Let's face it—with parents, there's typically a good cop and a bad cop. Dad's the cop who helps little old ladies cross the street. Mom's the cop who tickets them for jaywalking. So you know in advance which cop you want to run to and plead your case. But every now and then, you just need the cop who helps you through an emergency.

"Mom didn't get all scary, like I thought she would," Liv acknowledges. "She listened, and was ... *there*. She actually got where I was coming from. Who knew?"

Exactly. This day has been full of trippy surprises. Between my family, William's family, and Liv's potential family, things aren't automatically what you expect them to be—even when you have no idea what to expect. Because they manage to work themselves out, in ways you never saw coming, but somehow feel like the answer.

Who knew?

15

LAST HURRAH

DAY FIVE (Part One): Friday.

They say, "Three's a crowd."

I don't know if that's true. I don't even know who "they" are. But sometimes, it's just easier to attribute certain ideologies to unknown parties, so if the theory blows up in your face, you can hang it on "them." It's a total dick move, and really shouldn't be allowed when trying to make a point. That's what they say, anyway.

For the last week, it's only been the three of us—me, Dad and William—in our own small crowd. Well, in the down time, that is, when we weren't dodging nutjobs. But today, it's going to be a group of people, who all knew William and spent time with him, and who'll be coming together to remember him and will surely be staring at us in disbelief, figuring that a computer glitch must have enabled us onto the guest list.

Considering that we almost ruined, spilled, or impounded whatever's left of him, it was super generous of Helen to invite us to William's service. Talk about granting some latitude. That's the problem. I just can't get over the thought that we—or rather, *I*—don't deserve to be there, among William's family and friends. I'm not family. And after all the ridiculous things I've done to him, I doubt that William would want to be friends. So other than the fact that we were traveling companions, what right do I have to be at his funeral?

Now that we've gone and bought me a dress and all, I don't even know if I should tell Dad that I'm having second thoughts. But I don't want to go and have a meltdown and make a scene that will cause Dad even more humiliation than I've already put him through. That's not fair to him or William.

But if I don't go, is that like the final slap in the face to both of them? Insulting William and his family by not honoring this man who gave so much to others? And what about Dad? Would it be beyond selfish of me to suggest that he go on his own, and I'll just meet him afterward? Would that much social pressure just shove him further back into the shell he just crawled out of? The dilemma of it all is way too much to process, and since I'm not old enough to drink, my only choice is to sit here and hope that a tornado blows through town and everyone is evacuated, and then I can pretend to have scheduling issues when the funeral comes around again.

Does that sound awful? It does, doesn't it? That's unbelievably awful of me. I'm an awful person. And you're in my head. Which makes you a party to my awfulness, so you should be ashamed, too. Not really, but I'm just trying to share the blame. Get over it.

Oh joy, now Dad's come outside onto the motel balcony, where I'm wallowing in stress mode.

"What are you doing out here?" he asks.

I don't know if I should tell him. After all, what good is it going to do? It's not going to change anything ... other than taking the weight off my mind to tell him the truth, and give him and William the respect that I haven't shown through this entire trip. Which is the least I can do. So maybe it's time I did.

"I'm not sure I'll belong there. At William's service."

"Why not?" Dad poses.

"Because he made all these plans," I assert. "You know, he arranged to get himself here, because he didn't want to burden his family. He brought the stuff he wanted buried with him. He even brought his cat. How fantastic is that? That even now, he's still looking out for her."

Yes, it is fantastic. *William* was fantastic. And that's why I'm flipping out.

"But he didn't plan on some ding dong like me, and all the asinine things I put him through. So why would he want me at his service?"

"Because that's who he was," Dad encourages. "You heard what Helen said."

"But I'm not part of his plans. I shouldn't pretend to be."

Dad gives me one of those "parent" looks—you know, the ones where they're ready to knock some sense into you, but they get it that you're too wigged out to be manhandled. So he treads lightly.

"You know, the night I met your mom," he starts, "I was sitting in a café, near campus. I'd been stood up by a blind date."

Bitch.

"It wasn't fun," Dad remembers. "Felt like the entire place was staring at me. 'Look at that poor loser, sitting alone.' So I was getting ready to leave, and then your mom walked through the door. She looked so beautiful, and she smiled at me. My heart skipped a beat, wondering if she was the girl I was supposed to be meeting. She wasn't. But it turns out ... she was."

Huh? Oh no, don't tell me we're going down a Grandma road. I can't hop onto that crazy train right now. Just run me over, instead.

"Her face and her eyes were so ... bright, and warm. That was exactly what I needed to see at that moment. A kind face, to make me feel like I wasn't alone. And just like that, a stranger gave me back the confidence that another stranger had taken away."

"So what'd you do?" I ask.

"I figured we shouldn't be strangers anymore, so I talked to her. We ended up talking for the next two hours. And I decided that night, that I was going to marry her. I didn't know when or how I would convince her. All I knew is that she gave me some of the best moments of my life that night, and I wanted those moments to continue. Forever. But I never would have realized that if she hadn't walked through the door and smiled at me."

Like Grandma's theories, I know there's a point to all of this. But unlike Grandma's theories, Dad proceeds to tell me the point ... which is super handy, since I'm totally wiped.

"Sometimes, it's the people we don't plan on who change our lives."

Wow. So that's what it feels like to get actual advice? Even more astonishing is the idea that Dad—the zombified, bedhead, bathrobe loving, grave-digging anomaly of the last few months—is the one who's giving the advice. And the most shocking thing of all? *He's making sense.*

"Helen said that William would want you there," Dad assures. "And I believe her. Maybe you should, too."

I've got to hand it to Dad. If ever there were a perfect time to emerge from his neurotic hole, I'd say he nailed it. Between rescuing my brainless butt yesterday, when I was lost in so many ways, to being my shrink today, he came through when I absolutely needed him. Just like Helen said: "That's what good parents do."

That's why I get into the van and ride with Dad to the service. And as we arrive ...

I'm doing a double take at all of the cars in the parking lot, and cars lining the street. Is there another funeral going on at the same time? Or are all of these people here for William? Could it be?

Once we get inside, I realize ... it is. A room packed full of people, all gathering for William. I look around in awe, seeing that there was no need to worry. William had friends. Lots of friends, and he will be remembered. And for the first time on this entire trip, it feels like we've arrived at a real destination.

And even more unexpected, some of these faces look familiar. Not just Helen and her mom and that wingnut Cid. But other faces. *Small-town* faces, like ...

"Hey!" Lola waves from across the room. She nudges Charlene, who sits next to her.

"Oh, hi!" Charlene waves.

Sitting next to them are the mechanics from the electric car fiasco, who even cleaned up for the day ... if you can call it that. Surrounding them are some of the dance partners from the flash mob. Speaking of which—

"You made it!"

I turn around to see the dorkiest friendly face.

"I wasn't sure if you'd still be here," Linus says. "But I'm glad you are."

I don't know if it's Linus's goofy grin—with braces as big as train tracks—or just the fact that he cared enough to attend, but I'm stoked to see him.

"What are you doing here?" I ask.

"Well, I kept thinking about our talk, and I just wanted to make sure that William wouldn't be alone. So I put the word out, and a bunch of us carpooled overnight to get here."

There are some things people do that leave you speechless. Sometimes in a bad way, or a shocking way. But sometimes in this way, when they go so above and beyond, that no words can really do them justice.

"That's ... amazing," I gape at him.

Linus shrugs, humbled. "We wanted to do it."

Like I said, there are no words. Unless you count the *bad* words.

"Where's the food?" Walter bullishly interrupts. "There's usually food."

Unfortunately for us, Walter awoke from his sugar coma long enough to smell a free meal and drag himself away from the front desk. He notices me and seethes, "Ugh, it's *you*."

Oh yeah, I got words now. I don't frequently spit when I talk, although at this moment, I wish it were a habit.

"If I knew you were coming, I'd have baked a cake," I sneer at him, "And *ate it* right in front of you."

Linus tries to keep the peace, reassuring Walter, "We can get you something on the way back."

"You mean I gotta sit here for an hour with no food?"

Linus digs into his pocket. "I have some Tic Tacs."

"Stop enabling him!" I spout.

Linus caves and hands the dispenser to Walter, who gripes, "It's not even half full."

I'm so over this guy. Minty fresh or not, you can't dress up revulsion. So I don't.

"If penguins can cross the Arctic feeding off their flab, you can suck yours up for an hour," I insist.

While I'd bet that Walter had a dim grasp of anatomy to begin with, his body fat ratio has hopelessly slowed his response time. So Linus dives in to save the whale.

"Walter, why don't you take a seat?"

"Get one by the door, in case your water breaks," I goad.

Walter's teensy brain manages to process that one as an insult.

"I should have charged you for three people," he snottily retorts.

"Too bad you can't count that high," I shoot back.

"C'mon, kids!" Linus interjects. "Play nice now. It's not about us. We're here for William."

Walter tenses, as Linus holds up a stifling hand.

"—And food," Linus reassures.

Walter lumbers off, as I cast Linus a dirty look. My warm, fuzzy feeling of a few minutes ago has deteriorated faster than the guest list.

"When you sent the 'word' out, exactly what word did you send?"

"Cellmate!" a dreaded voice arises.

You know how I said I'm gonna stop asking if things can get worse, because that just opens the door for the universe to prove they can? Apparently, I need to stop thinking it, too, considering what's now standing in front of me.

"Well, not legally, since it didn't involve bail," the clown chuckles, before admitting, "Not for you, anyway."

Remember when you were little and you were taught that it's not polite to stare, no matter how desperately you might want to? You know what I'm talking about. Every kid invariably gets that teaching moment. Yeahhh …

I flunked that lesson.

"Hey, glad he made it in one piece," the clown rambles. "Little awkward to have a funeral without the guest of honor."

The clown snorts, amused, as I shoot Linus a glare of disgust.

"*Explain*," I demand.

Linus flinches, embarrassed. "I didn't recognize him until we were halfway here. I'd never seen him without his makeup."

Yes, you heard right. The clown is now *au naturale*, without the face paint and bulbous nose. Even though his hair is still something of a rat's nest—sort of a homemade, off-kilter mullet—it looks like a comb may have been in the vicinity at one point. And his outfit can only be described as grossly inappropriate, although a feeble step up from the usual. Let's be real—a green velvet tux, chartreuse ruffled shirt, and white platform shoes arguably have their own place in the world ... but it's more like a Leprechaun prom, rather than a funeral. The clown, however, was absent on the day of that fashion lesson. So here we are. Or simply put, here *he* is, wearing *that*. But wait! There's more ...

"I'm thinking of becoming a mime," the clown announces. "You know, still along the clown lines, but classier. What do you think?"

I think *I've* become a mime, since I've lost the ability to speak. I know this guy tokes a lot, but c'mon, how fried does your brain have to be to assume that there's a "classy" version of clowns? I don't even know how to dignify this numbnuts with a response. Linus's method is to dig up some highbrow words.

"How avant-garde. An eloquent and impassioned conveyance through fluid improvisation and sans articulation."

The clown's eyeballs freeze like a pair of fogged-up goggles. Good thing he has a backup plan, because "intellectual" is clearly off the list. I try to keep things— namely Leonard the Clown—moving along.

"Hey, you should grab a seat," I prompt. "There's probably half of one open next to Walter."

I flutter one of those "shooing" motions—the kind of gesture that impatient relatives make to an annoying child. Turns out, the clown is versed in pantomime, after all, since he mercifully catches on and shuffles off into the crowd. At least he's out of my hair and perhaps onto a new career, if Linus doesn't kill it first.

"Are you out of your mind?" I scold Linus. "He's finally ready to do everybody a favor and shut up, and you scare him with big words!"

"I know, I'm sorry," Linus cowers. "I just didn't know what to say about the whole 'mime' thing, because there can't be much career opportunity with it. But if he sees it as creative expression, then that's a positive and should be encouraged. Plus, when I get nervous I tend to over-verbalize."

Leave it to the egghead. When most people spit stuff out in an awkward moment, it's generally curse words or the name of their ex. Linus gushes advanced vocabulary.

And just when it appears we've tapped out the wackos in the room, an itsy-bitsy spider tugs at my skirt.

"I'm supposed to tell you there's a seat for you, over by the family," Cid sourly passes along. "Don't know why, but it's there."

I look to see Helen waving me over to a seat next to Dad. And yes, it is near the family, which visibly irks Cid.

"No funny business," he snarls. "I got my eye on you."

In a normal world, the image of a self-professed bodyguard with anger management issues could be disconcerting. But since we've only been able to see the normal world in the distance this past week, I'm hardly buying Cid's veiled threat. Especially since his eye is barely at my hip level.

"So say goodbye to your boyfriend," Cid spouts. "Keep it short."

Cid tromps off as that pesky snicker builds in my throat again. I can't lose it at a funeral. Even Linus is trying to control a bit of a smirk, and if *he* can't maintain composure, I don't have a prayer. Time to divide and conquer. I quickly head over to Dad, as Linus sits with Lola and Charlene. The clown squirms into the ever-shrinking seat next to Walter.

And here we go, on the last leg of this far-out journey to bring William home. It's already taken us to worlds I never would have sought out otherwise ... and somehow brought us to a place that found us.

Until today, I've only been to two funerals. One was for my grandma, and the other was for Petey, my hamster—although, that was more improvised, since it was in my bedroom. There wasn't, like, an organ or anything. I tried to play "Taps" on a harmonica. Problem is, I don't know how to play the harmonica, so it sounded more like gas in search of a melody.

But this ... this is wild. I'm at a funeral for someone I didn't genuinely know, although I feel like I know him, and I vaguely know his family, and they must feel like they sort of know us to have invited us here, along with other friends I don't know but who seem to know his family, so they had to have known William, even though I have no idea who they are and they don't know me, which means they certainly don't know Linus and the locals and, like the rest of us, have no desire whatsoever to know Walter or the clown ... you know?

What's even more of a trip, but surprisingly comforting, are the pictures of William, which are gathered around his urn. A part of me secretly wanted to keep the vision in my head, even though it was more nondescript, and was more about William's essence than his face. But seeing his face —smiling, laughing, alongside his family and friends—reminds me that William, truly, had a life. A full life, with moments that were celebrated and treasured. Moments that will be remembered.

There are pictures of him as a child, with a woman who must be his mother. A beautiful woman, holding him close, as only a mother can. There are photos of William as a teenager, hanging out with Helen and her family, and a prepubescent Cid (which is every bit as scary as it sounds). Pictures from his high school yearbook, his college graduation, and his early days as a paramedic; shots of him receiving awards and commendations, and gathered with friends and coworkers at football games, parties, and on vacations. Photos show William skiing, hiking, running and out on his mountain bike. Images of laughter, joy, and boundless appreciation for a rich and valued life.

But amongst all of these images, there is one that I can't take my eyes off of. One that is so special, so touching, so honest, it brings a hollow feeling to my throat: the picture of William's strong arms gently cradling the precious, innocent life that was Delilah. Yes, she was beautiful—just as Helen described. And William's obvious care and regard for her are visible in every inch of his face and touch, leaving no question that she was his best friend.

Now the box with her ashes rests next to his urn. The little box with the words "Bee" and "Live" painted on the top and bottom. I still don't get that part, but I fully get why she's here and why William wanted her at his side. Some people might think it's "girly" that a guy loved his cat so much. You've heard about the "Crazy Cat Lady," but there's no real name for guys who like cats, so people wrongly assume they must be a wuss.

But looking at these photos, it's obvious that William was no wuss. He was tough, and accomplished and brave. He was everything you'd want from the person to whom you'd entrusted your life. And loving something so small and fragile only made him stronger, because he didn't care what anyone thought about it. You gotta hand it to him. We live in an age of public scrutiny and social bashing aimed to tear people down every day. So to have the determination to live your life, and be who you are and not agonize about the blowback—that's *real* strength.

That's why I look over at Linus, sitting with the locals who drove overnight to come here and honor a man they didn't know. Sure, technically, Walter doesn't count in that mix since he's only here for the buffet. But Linus does count—because he lives his geeky life in all its dweebed out, adorable glory, and is totally on board with that. And so are the people who came with him, who are all living on their own margins, in one way or another. But they care, and they show up. And if that's the best we get from the people around us, that's pretty damn good.

Helen tentatively steps up to the podium. "I've never been the one who's good at public speaking. But since we're waiting for that person, I guess I'll start."

Helen searches for the right words, attesting, "Big brothers can be annoying."

A collective laugh runs throughout the room.

"But they can also be the one person you want by your side, when times get rough ... knowing that they'll protect you, defend you, and help you get back up when you fall."

Cid chokes back a cough, but unlike my usual cackles, his is not from laughter. I glance at him and notice that he's holding back a tear. Wow—maybe he's not entirely a soulless little troll, after all.

"Billy was a protector. He stood up for his family and friends, and fought for those he didn't even know. He saved lives and enriched so many along the way. And when he came to live with us ..."

A door creaks open in the lobby, as Helen continues, "He gave me the blessing of two big brothers. And I have never felt more safe ... more protected."

Helen catches the eye of the person who has just entered. The room turns to see her tall, husky brother Barry, who removes the hat of his military dress uniform. I'm not sure where he came from, or how long he'd been away, but it was enough that he fights to hold his composure as he walks down the aisle and tightly hugs his sister.

"It's all good, baby," he assures. "I'm home."

Helen looks up and whispers—possibly to Barry, or to someone else—"Thank you."

Barry then leans down and gives his mother a tender hug and kiss. From her wheelchair, his mom looks up at her son and smiles—the fog in her mind lifting long enough to give them this moment.

Helen returns to the podium. "Like I said, I'm not very good at this, so I'll turn it over to someone who is. My dear, sweet giant of a brother, Barry."

Barry collects himself and steps up before the crowded room. He looks to the urn and gives it a gentle fist bump. I can't help but picture William returning the sentiment. Barry swallows hard, taking a long, deep breath.

"Billy was my brother, in every sense of the word," he begins. "Even though we weren't born of the same parents, he was my blood. And there was absolutely nothing that either one of us wouldn't have done for the other. Because that's what brothers do. They take charge. They take care. And they bring you home."

I glance over to Dad, who silently hangs his head. I feel like I should say something reassuring, but since we're at a funeral, it would be pretty tacky to start talking—and considering that we've been straddling the boundaries of good taste throughout this trip, perhaps a touch of class should prevail. So I take his hand, instead. Turns out, that's all that needs to be said.

Barry pauses, deep in thought. "When Billy first told me he was sick, I wanted to race home and be there for my brother. Try to power through this thing. Beat it down. I wanted to protect him, because he deserved that. He deserved someone having his back. But I had a job to do. I had troops depending on me, and even though there were oceans and deserts between us, Billy knew that I was right by his side. Whenever we'd get the chance to talk, he'd tell me, 'Be strong out there.' And I'd tell him …" Barry holds a fist to his heart, "Be strong in here."

I can hear Helen softly crying, as I watch her and her mother, sitting amongst a group of what must be William's extended family. Fellow paramedics sit behind them, each with a black armband on their uniform. Scanning their faces, it's undeniable that all of these people loved William very much, and he had a real impact on their lives.

My eyes drift back to the pictures of him, and I realize how alive he still is—through memories, through the work he did to save others, and through the people in this room. They all knew William. His face, his voice, his laugh. His presence.

"Anybody who knew Billy knew he usually got in the last word. It doesn't mean he didn't listen to people ... just means he had a way to make you hear him, even when you thought the conversation was over."

Barry then opens an envelope that sits on the podium.

"Even now, Billy has some things to say, so he asked us to read this letter for you all."

I can feel my heart racing a bit. Up until now, I've only seen William, but haven't actually heard him. Oh no, what if it changes my mind about him? What if he's a dick with bad grammar? What if he's shallow and condescending? What if his words are scathing, full of judgment and tirades about how dumb and irritating people are? What if he sounds like the incessant conversations in my head, and ultimately sounds like ... *ME???*

Okay, point taken. I'll shut up now.

Barry gently unfolds the paper and clears his throat. He begins reading ...

Hi everyone. It's probably no surprise that I'm not going quietly into my new life. You can't shut me up that easily. As I've often done, I'm standing in front of a breathtaking horizon, calling out to see if my voice comes back. I've realized it has a few more things to say …

First of all, I want to thank each of you, for the time that you have given me; for every day past, and every day to come, by allowing a little bit of me to live on in you. Time is one of the most precious things we have, and I am so honored to have shared some of ours together.

The truth in any lifetime is that not all days are easy. But every day, every moment, matters. Through my work, I have learned the delicate balance of joy and sadness, sometimes separated by a single breath. I have cradled the bodies of newborns, and those of dying souls, feeling the miracle of life in my hands. It is those moments that have helped me to understand and appreciate all of the moments in-between. I may not have had a conventional life, but it was all mine, and it was meant to be.

I was brought into this world by two extraordinary parents, and was privileged to be raised by a third. I was not born into a family of brothers and sisters, but was lucky enough to have one of each. I did not marry, but had countless soul mates in the wonderful friends who have been at my side. I did not have children, but was blessed to adopt the most beautiful little girl, who just happened to be covered in fur. She opened my mind and my heart, giving me the most unconditional love in return. And although my body became sick, it did not fail me, because it gave me decades to explore and climb and play, and be strong enough to lift up others who needed help, and carry us both to safety.

So on this final journey, I am taking what I can carry in my heart. And with all of the love I have been blessed to know in my life, my heart is absolutely full. My mother and father were a testament to what love can endure. My adopted family embodies what love can become. And all of you here today are the destinations that I was meant to find. You made me so much better than I might have been otherwise. On your road ahead, I wish you safe travels, a song in your heart, and joy beyond measure.

Most of all, I hope that your steps along your journey take you to the most sublime and extraordinary place you'll ever know ... to the very best part of yourself. I could never predict those times when I managed to get there, because life led the way. So when you arrive, just open your eyes, take it all in, then do whatever you can to remember that sacred place, and let it inform who you are. It is the earthly breath of where I will see you again one day.

Until then, always remember that I'm not far away. Just call out, wherever you are, and my voice will find its way back to you—in memories, in laughter, in stillness, and maybe even by surprise. Because one thing I'm sure of: there is no distance great enough that we won't hear each other. I promise you that.

So now I sign off, with the honor of the name that makes me most proud. The name I inherited from my father...

William Thomas Parkner.

There it is: William's voice. He's not who I had hoped he'd be. He's so much more. I don't know what I did these last few days that I deserve to be here. But whatever it was, it introduced me to William. The *real* William. Not an urn of ashes, not a prop, not an inanimate object ... but a living spirit that is in every inch of this room.

And that was absolutely worth my spring break.

16

LAST CHANCE

DAY FIVE (Part Two): Still Friday.

"Bee." "Live."

I stare at the box with Delilah's ashes and can't help but be curious about the words painted upon it. But maybe the words are a piece of William's puzzle meant to stay private. So part of me doesn't want to bring it up, even when Helen comes over.

"I'm glad you came today," she gives me a warm pat on the shoulder. "I wish you could have known him in life. He was something."

"Seems like he was very special," I remark.

"He was. But I think you already knew that."

My eyes drift back over to the little box, as Helen notices my interest.

"Billy's mom called him 'Bee,'" Helen explains. "He had a little yellow blanket with black stripes, and when he was wrapped up, he looked like a bumblebee. Remember how I said he and Barry were called 'The King Bees?' That's until they got into trouble. Then they'd suck up and became 'The Honey Bees.'"

She laughs at the memory. "Billy made this box in wood shop. Then his mom painted the words on it. She told him to always remember that good things can come out of any situation."

Helen's finger traces the letters of "Bee" and "Live" as she continues, "That sometimes, all you have to do is make one small change to create something new."

She opens the lid of the box, revealing the word painted inside: BELIEVE.

"Billy wasn't sure what was beyond this life. But he believed that love would be waiting for him, and show him the way."

I wouldn't describe myself as overly weepy, but something about this moment just makes me want to hug Helen. So I do. And she does something so unexpected, it takes a little bit of my breath away. She pats the back of my head, which is the same thing my grandma used to do. A gentle pat to reassure a child that everything's going to be okay.

A week ago, I wouldn't have expected to end up here. But somehow, this whole dingbat trip feels like it led to just the right place ... to an embrace that feels like family.

Dad comes over to us, as Helen reaches out her hand to him.

"We're so grateful for all you've done," she warmly conveys.

Dad blushes, embarrassed. "I just did my job."

Helen fondly smiles, enjoying a cherished memory. "That's what Billy used to say."

Helen moves along to greet other guests, as Dad and I look around the crowded room.

"He was very admired," Dad comments.

"Yeah," I agree. "I'd never get this many flowers."

"Why do you say that?"

"My generation doesn't send flowers. We send emails and texts. I might get virtual flowers from Linus, but I wouldn't hold out hope for the real thing. I mean, look at this …"

I start reading the cards aloud.

"*'With deepest sympathies, Aunt Elsie and Uncle George.'* They're obviously from a generation that sends flowers."

"Stop reading those," Dad cautions.

I ignore his pleas. "*'Our thoughts are with you, The Blake family.'* See, that's smart. The family designates one person to maintain decorum and sign on their behalf, because if they left it up to the kids, they'd get an e-card."

"Those are none of our business!" Dad frets again, sounding like a broken record.

"They're on public view," I note. "Chill."

He sighs as I go down the line, catching a glimpse of another signature. I stop cold, before ticking my head, "Dad …?"

He looks over as I hold out the card. Dad chokes up, upon seeing: *"Our sincerest condolences in your time of sorrow. With deepest respect, The Sarazen Family."*

William said it himself, that time is one of the most precious things we have. And amidst all the craziness of a Bridezilla wedding, a florist in Boulder took the time to acknowledge a life she never knew, but a life that she knew had touched her family.

Dad speed dials his phone.

"Hi Sally," he lovingly says.

Dad steps aside to talk to Mom, as I notice Helen's mother, sitting quietly in her wheelchair. Something makes me go over to her—although I'm not really sure what to say, since I've only met her once. Well, I didn't even technically meet her, since she was sleeping most of the time that I was at the care home. The couple of times she did wake up, she was a bit … "fuzzy." I never asked Helen what was going on with her. For once, I willingly went along with Dad's mantra about not prying. When somebody gets fuzzy like that, you can't get too picky about details. You just have to go with it.

"We haven't officially met. I'm Greer."

She gives me a sweet grin, "I'm Sunny."

An awkward pause, before I offer, "It was a very nice service."

"Oh yes, it was," Sunny perks up. "I'm so glad Billy made it in time."

Ooh … I know I said that I was going to go with the fuzziness, but under the circumstances, I feel like I need to speak up.

"You mean, 'Barry,' your son," I presume.

"No, *Billy*," she affirms. "My godson. Didn't you see him walk in?"

Hang on … I agree that urn has done some offbeat things these past few days, but let's be realistic. Even crab walking would be a stretch.

"He came in and sat next to me," Sunny proudly boasts. "And held my hand."

Who knows if it's the fuzziness talking, but whatever is making her say these words, she clearly believes them. So I indulge her.

"That's nice," I reply, then look around. "Is he still ... *here?*"

"He had to leave. Had someplace he had to be. I don't know what that boy was talkin' about. But maybe you can catch up with him another time."

I smile at the thought. "I'd like that."

We sit quietly until Linus comes over, profusely apologizing for the interruption.

"Oh, don't mind, child," Sunny says, nudging me, "Young love needs attention."

"*Huh??*" Linus gulps.

"Don't take it personally," I console him.

"But the dwarf thought I was your boyfriend, too."

"Yeah, but he's delusional by choice," I dismiss. "What's up?"

"We're going to be heading back. After we stop at Waffle House."

"Ooh, I love me some waffles," Sunny pipes up.

Wow, *she* tuned in.

"There's a reception, you know," I inform Linus.

"They gonna have waffles?" Sunny anxiously beams.

Good Lord—it's like hearing myself at eighty-five.

"I'm sure it's okay if you stayed," I urge Linus.

"I know," he says. "I'm just afraid of a public spectacle. Plus, Leonard just informed me there's a warrant out for him in Michigan. He can't quite recall what it's for, but assumes it's still active. We have to get back over state lines."

"You'd think he would have mentioned that before coming here," I snidely critique.

"He forgot," Linus winces.

"How do you 'forget' an arrest warrant??"

"You'd be surprised," Sunny huffs.

Not that I'm against her chiming in—since it's oddly entertaining—but I have no idea how much of this she's actually processing. Linus, meanwhile, swims in a sea of paranoia.

"Until the rodeo, the closest I'd come to being arrested was when I snuck off to school with the chicken pox, because I wanted to keep up my perfect attendance record. They called my mom to take me home, but I was still forcibly removed."

"Forced to miss school? How devastating," I dryly taunt.

"It scarred me more than the chicken pox," Linus concurs, not catching on.

Under normal circumstances, I'd say Linus needs to get out more. But considering that in the last two days, he's played footsie with a bull, been questioned by the police, joined a flash mob, and is now road-tripping with a fugitive, maybe it's time to give him a pass.

"You're all right, Linus," I conclude. "Kinda bizarre, but all right."

"When are you going to accept that that's not my name?" he sighs.

"Really? This again?" I reprimand him. "*Linus* ..."

"*Greer*," he shoots back.

On that note, I decide that William's mom may have been right—that one small change can mean finding the good in any situation. In my case, rearranging the letters just confused things, so it could be that the good is found in what was there all along. Like William, maybe I should welcome the name given to me by my parents.

"Greer," I repeat. "I guess it's not so bad."

"I like it," Linus smugly maintains.

He then gives me a hug. Even though Linus is a stick figure, his toothpick arms still make me feel secure, which is what you want in a friend. Although, some people see what they want to see.

"Look at that," Sunny gushes. "Young love."

AND we're done. Linus and I break our hug so fast you'd think somebody yelled "Unfriend!!"

"Thank you," Linus says. "Now I have to go take another bewildering trip."

He heads toward the door, when I call out to him—

"Hey, if you outlive me, would you send virtual flowers to my funeral?"

Linus ponders the request, then grins. "Kinda bizarre … but, all right."

"Cool," I say, as Linus waves goodbye.

It is cool, to know that somebody out there has your back. Although, right now, somebody down there has my kneecap, as Cid pokes my leg.

"Food's up," he grouses. "In the other room."

I toss him a smirk, just because I can. "Thanks."

Cid glares at me, suspiciously waiting for more. It's like a Mexican standoff, except my opponent is so far south of the border, we eventually call it a draw.

Cid's stout arms strain to reach the handles of Sunny's wheelchair.

"C'mon, Sunny," Cid announces. "I'll take you."

Sunny shoots me a look of concern, mumbling, "Lord, have mercy."

"Hey Cid," I pipe up. "Nice suit."

Cid gives me a wary once-over, spouting, "That's it? What, you're not gonna make some snarky comment? Like, 'Oh gee, looks like the Big and Tall shop was sold out.' C'mon, bring it on!"

I hold a beat, fighting my more cynical side from taking the bait. Finally, I acquiesce, "It looks good on you. The suit works."

Cid narrows his brow, incredulous. I just hold a straight face. As he turns away, I add:

"... Not so puffy."

"There it is!" Cid hisses. "You can't let even the *tiniest* thing go!"

Oh God, help me. Breathe, breathe ...

Cid pushes Sunny's chair, shooting me the evil eye and bumping into things as they make their way. Seriously, it's like watching the Headless Horseman drive a scooter. From that angle, objects are much closer than they appear. But one object does grab Cid's attention.

He passes the photo of him and William, and pauses for a moment. I inquisitively watch Cid, as he privately wipes a tear. Even though my pessimistic self would say it's for show, something tells me that this is for real. Apart from anything Cid may have done wrong in his life, revering William is one thing he got right. And that's huge ... even if Cid isn't.

Sunny looks at the photos of William and plants a gentle kiss onto her fingers, which she presses against his image. Who knows how much she comprehends about what happened here, or why so many people gathered for her godson.

But one thing she's right about: William was here today. In so many ways.

*

At the reception, I watch as people chat, laugh, and reminisce about their brother, their cousin, their friend. Even though I have memories with William, part of me feels like I can't openly talk about them. Not with others, anyway. Not even with Dad. Because what happened with William and me was not anything I ever expected, or prepared for, or ... wanted, even. At least that's what I thought a week ago. But now, I realize that those moments will never happen again, with anyone. Not in the same way. So I seek out the one person I can honestly talk to; the one person who will understand.

"It wasn't really *that* shallow," I contend, as I sit next to William's urn, beside the plot of ground where his and Delilah's ashes will be buried, next to the grave of his mother. "I mean, it's not like I *wanted* to see that hillbilly choke, because I probably would have had to give a statement, which would have just delayed everything, so when Charlene smacked him, it was pretty much a win-win, right?"

The gravedigger—the one who works at *this* cemetery—perks up an ear as he works nearby.

"Sorry, I know you've got work to do here," I say. "My dad does this work, too, so I get it. What you guys do is important ... even if it bums people out."

He silently agrees, as I add, "I'll be done soon."

"Take your time," he says.

The gravedigger politely steps away as I turn back to William's urn.

"I was trying to think of something ... I don't know ... *poetic* ... to say, since this'll be our last time together. I'm still working on it."

I look around, taking in the scenery. "I'm glad your family will get to visit you here. It's nice. Not a bad place to hang out."

I consider Delilah's little box, which rests next to William.

"And you'll be with the ones you love."

I study his mom's headstone, and the memorial marker for William's dad. In that moment, it hits me that there is no grave for his father, since—like Helen said—there was nothing to bury. But the physical remains are just one part of a person's existence, because what truly *remains* are the memories of those we love. And that's something that can't be taken away.

"I don't know if I'll get back here to visit again," I concede. "I can try, but I just don't know when it would be. And if it's too long, you might forget about me, and then ... well, that'd be awkward."

I gently touch William's urn.

"But I'll never forget you, William," I promise. "I wish I could have known you in life. But I'm at least glad I got to know you now. You're all right."

I lift the lid of his urn, gazing at the baggie with his ashes.

"Kinda bizarre, but all right."

I hear someone come up behind me. Since I can still see the gravedigger out of the corner of my eye, I figure it must be the *other* gravedigger. The one I live with. But I don't turn around just yet, because there's something left to say.

I lightly stroke the box with Delilah's ashes.

"I'm glad you'll keep him company, little girl." To my own surprise, I start to choke up, as I add, "So he's not alone."

Suddenly, I feel loving arms wrapping me in their embrace, as Dad sits beside me while I cry. He patiently comforts me, "It's okay. Let it out."

I begin to process that what scares me more than losing William, is the thought that I'm going to face more of these moments as I get older.

"Is this what it's like?" I ask. "When people die?"

"You remember losing your grandma," Dad reminds.

"I know, but ..." I struggle to find the words. "She was old, and sick, and ... she was ready to go. But William ... he wasn't that old. He should still be here. Shouldn't he?"

Dad gives me a long, thoughtful look, trying to make sense of all of this.

"From what we've learned about him, he made the most of every day," Dad surmises. "That's all any of us can do, at any age. And he had a lifetime full of people who loved him. That's all any of us can hope for."

"At any age," I softly add.

"At any age," Dad echoes.

We share a hug, as I notice the gravedigger watching and wiping his eyes.

"C'mon," Dad nudges. "We should get going. We've got a long drive back."

Almost unconsciously, I wonder aloud, "Is it strange that I'm gonna miss him?"

"No," Dad replies. "A part of me will miss him, too."

"The part named William?"

Dad laughs. "Yeah."

I cast one final look to the urn.

"Goodbye, William," I say, composing myself. "I'm sorry if our trip was pretty ridiculous. But I hope you had some fun. I did. I'll miss you."

I turn and take a few steps, then look back to notice Dad pausing for a moment.

"Goodbye," Dad whispers.

And just like that ... a gentle breeze stirs up, out of nowhere. Just distinct enough to make its presence felt. I think I may have even heard ... *something*. I can't be sure. Dad and I stop and look at each other. Whatever it was, he heard it, too.

And just like that ... we understand. We're not the only ones who said goodbye.

As we walk away, Dad and the resident gravedigger exchange respectful nods, each acknowledging what the other has done to bring William home.

And what a beautiful home it is.

17

AT LAST

"I've lost my will to live," Grandma said.

"What?" Mom reacted, shocked. "When?"

"Yesterday. I was reading it, and now I can't find the damn thing."

One blank look later—

"You mean your 'living will'?" Mom surmised.

An even longer blank look—

"I'm living *where??*" Grandma asked, puzzled.

Toward the end, conversations like that became the norm ... which is a little weird, considering that "weird" became the "norm." But it did. I gotta admit, that one was especially entertaining, mostly because of what followed: when Mom started laughing and put her arms around Grandma.

"I love you, Mama," she said.

I remember that scene like it was yesterday. Because in my mind, it was. Maybe that's where all of our most special memories live ... just around a corner in our mind. We look back, peek around, and catch sight of them peeking at us. And we smile, knowing that they're never far away.

Even Sunny seemed to know that, even when she couldn't look back anymore. Her heart still recognized what mattered, because that awareness lived in a protected place, where love wouldn't let anything touch it. That's why she could feel William's presence next to her, no matter what form their connection took. She knew that William was there with her—for that moment, for that instant, forever. And that was all the clarity she needed.

I wonder if William may show up one day and just hang out with me for a while. Hey, it's hardly the most "off the wall" thing that could arise from all this. I mean, if someone had told me that I'd spend my spring break babysitting an urn, hanging with a geek, having stare-downs with hillbillies, running my ass off at a rodeo, "sort of" getting arrested, disco dancing in the middle of nowhere, getting chased by a belligerent dwarf, crashing an old folks' home and going to a stranger's funeral, I would have said they'd gone off the deep end.

That's what I would have said at first. But looking back, now I'd say something else. Now I'd say ...

I wasn't just babysitting an urn. I was giving Dad the time he needed to find himself, to lift him out of his stupor.

I wasn't just hanging with a geek. I was befriending someone who deserves a friend ... and whatever his name is, at least he knows his own heart.

I wasn't just having stare-downs with hillbillies. I was standing my ground to protect what I believe ... that

William deserves to be treated like a person, regardless of what form he's in.

I wasn't just running my ass off at a rodeo. I was trying to right my own wrong, so that Dad wouldn't have to do it.

I wasn't just "sort of" getting arrested. I was taking responsibility for my actions, whether I wanted to or not.

I wasn't just disco dancing in the middle of nowhere. I was celebrating the spontaneity of life, and the moments that take us by surprise.

I wasn't just getting chased by a belligerent dwarf. I was being given an opportunity to understand someone who's spent his life being misunderstood.

I wasn't just crashing an old folks' home. I was going the extra mile for someone I care about.

And I wasn't going to a stranger's funeral … because William was no longer a stranger. So, for him, I needed to do the honorable thing, because that's what he would have done.

In some way, I hope I was going to that destination that William talked about: to the very best part of myself. The center that lets me get back in touch with whatever I've lost. We all have that space inside of us. The place where we find our grace, our truth. Maybe getting there unconsciously is the only way to find it. The directions are the chances we're given to make a difference, to make an impact, to make something special out of every moment. And if we can live in that place for even just a little while, it reminds us of what we can truly be.

In the end, my spring break wasn't so bad, after all. Sure, I met some lunatics. But we all tread around the fringe of insanity at times, and life is about figuring out the steps. Some are big, some are small, but they all lead us to where we're meant to go. It turns out ...

Mom's kickass arrangements for the Bridezilla wedding got her a lot of good press, so business is picking up again. She's even been able to hire back a few employees, and they've been cranking away all summer.

Even though Dad was bracing to get fired after the whole road trip escapade, he ended up getting a raise, instead. It probably had something to do with the phone call from Helen, who told Digby that Dad cared about more than just doing a good job—he truly cared about the families he was serving, just like William did. And that made him the perfect person to transport her brother.

Digby was so impressed, he soon promoted Dad to head accountant in the main office, after their old accountant retired. No more gravedigging. Dad's back to digging into the books. I'd say he's back to his old self, but that's not quite true. He's better than his old self, because now his work has meaning, beyond what's on the page. Funny how it took death to bring him back to life.

As for me, I finally got my driver's license, and even a new appreciation for the Steaming Buddha. Despite my resistance, he did manage to open my teenage mind, which is sort of like opening a can of Spam—you're not too sure what's in it, but if it's the only thing on the shelf, you give it a whirl.

Along with parallel parking, the Buddha taught me that our thoughts and words have power. They can heal and they can harm; they can create and they can destroy. It's up to us how we use them. Maybe that's part of a teacher's job: waking us up to the person we are, in order to inform the person we become.

Considering that I've still got some topics to work on in the tact department, let me just add that I refuse to stop calling him "The Steaming Buddha," because it's simply too perfect. But I do use the term now with a new sense of endearment, since he is a big, sweaty pile of love. We should all be so lucky to know someone like that.

Then, of course, there are the little piles of love, who also become our teachers. The ones who open our eyes, our awareness, and our souls, in ways we never expected. They can be children, animals, or even someone in an urn. They make us conscious, force us to unplug, and remind us to live for today, without losing sight of tomorrow.

Liv can attest to that. By facing a massive decision, she learned that when you don't know the answer, it's usually best to listen to your heart. So she did, and heard two hearts: hers and her baby's. Without a doubt, she's terrified of being a parent. The potential for mucking it up is huge. And when factoring in the genes of her loser boyfriend, mucking it up is practically a birthright. But remember when I said that Liv loves stare-downs? Some of that resolve must have settled into another part of her brain, since she's getting a colossal eyeful of her future on the baby aisle, and isn't looking away.

I asked Liv what made her decide that motherhood wasn't such a bad thing for her. She said, "Our parents." Normally, I would have thought she was kidding. But something changed—for both of us—in how we see them. When Liv told Mom about her pregnancy, and instead of tearing her down, Mom lifted her up ... in that moment, something changed. And when Dad put his neck on the line for me, literally, by chasing a bull that could have pulverized us both ... something changed. Because they were doing the things that parents always do: coming to our rescue and saving us from ourselves. But for the first time, we truly *felt* them doing it, and appreciated them in a whole new way.

Liv doesn't know if she'll ever master those skills. Right now, she's just dealing with one freakout at a time. But at least she's willing to try. Maybe that means she's growing up. After all, she did stop bleeding.

And about that ... I'm still not exactly sure what Grandma meant. But I've determined that's the purpose of Grandma's advice. She didn't want me to know her meaning. She wanted me to find my own. And to do that, you sometimes have to go somewhere unexpected. Someplace that scares you, challenges you, and even hurts you.

But that same place can also inspire you, renew you, and eventually, make you whole again. Because when you find your way back, you stop bleeding. When you summon the strength to stand up, for yourself and for others, the pain begins to cease. When you nurture the gifts that were born within you, and embrace the chance to share those gifts, the wound begins to close. When you honor the legacies of those who've graced your life, by applying what they taught you, the scar begins to fade. Piece by piece, step by step, you find yourself anew. Because however bad things may seem at times, you're never beyond repair.

And once you realize that you have the power to heal yourself, just imagine what you could do out in the world.

Looking back on everything, it seems we've all done some growing up this past year. And I'm beginning to think that's how it's supposed to be. That maybe growing up isn't something we do all at once, or some invisible line we cross by a certain age. Maybe it's something that happens a little bit every day, no matter how old we are. That way, the wonder of being a child never really leaves us—it goes along for the ride. That'd be friggin' awesome.

Yeah ... I'm sticking with that. That's my meaning. I guess I'm lucky that it only took sixteen years to figure out.

At last.

Made in the USA
Middletown, DE
30 November 2018